Old Clothes

But All I Wanted to Do Was
Wear Old Clothes and Go Back to the Past

Perspectives of a Living Historian

Richard N. Pawling

Rich Pawling's History Alive!
224 Mail Route Road
Sinking Spring, PA 19608

www.richpawling.com

ISBN: 1463542194
ISBN-13: 978-1463542191

Cover Image by OODAX / C. Moore
Left to Right: Rich Pawling portraying -
Bucky Jones, Asa Brainard, the Author, L.B. Smith & Frank Kehoe
See page 37 for Living History Character Descriptions

DEDICATION

To my wife Diane. Without her love and support
my living history dream would never have become a reality.

CONTENTS

PREFACE

"If you don't know where you have come from, then you don't know who you are. And if you don't know who you are, then you have no idea where you are going." This quotation summarizes my philosophy about the value of understanding history and culture. Life is a journey and understanding our past plays an important role in helping us to continue to learn not only about life in general, but more importantly, about ourselves.

One approach to learn about history and culture (though not the only method) is to embrace it through the technique known as living history. The primary purpose for writing this book is to offer my perspectives on the proper methods of using this sometimes controversial means of portraying the past (in its various forms: first person, third person and spirit of the past interpretation). Unfortunately, it's not as simple as just "wearing old clothes and going back to the past."

The book begins by establishing a definition of living history. Having always believed that your personal history has a definitive influence on the way you interpret the past, the "journey" begins with my birth and travels throughout my life as I have continued (and still continue) to learn from life's experiences. These experiences include glimpses of "the good, the bad and the ugly" from my thirty plus years of involvement in the living history field.

Those readers who are contemplating getting involved in the field will find a detailed "how to" guide and practical advice about the process to follow to produce the best quality living historians. In addition, I cover perspectives about what living history research has taught me about my genealogy and my connections to America's story and conclude with an overview of the future of the profession and how to most effectively use living history to teach future generations about their past.

This book was written for all of us who live on Planet Earth (i.e., for everybody)! If you are employed as an interpretive park ranger or a naturalist, a museum or tour guide, or if you volunteer as a docent at a park, museum or historic site or are a reenactor - this book will be of particular interest. It's a book about me and a book about you. It covers the past, the present and the future. It's a book about life for as you'll discover (or rediscover) by reading it - **History is People!**

CHAPTER ONE

ARE YOU ONE OF THOSE LIVING DEAD PEOPLE?

"Are you two some of those living dead people?" she asked. I have heard of Jerry Garcia and the Grateful Dead, but, now we have the Living Dead - and, the last time I looked, I am not a brain-munching zombie. Still, the young girl who asked the question was on to something. Dr. T. Lindsay Baker and I, touring the Gettysburg National Battlefield in nineteenth century period civilian attire, must have looked like living dead people. I loved her question - a fitting place to begin this book.

That child's question deserves an answer. What is living history? Before we tackle this issue, we first must define the broader category under which living history falls: the field of interpretation. Like the translation of a foreign language, interpretation translates natural and cultural environments. The field includes living historians, naturalists, guides, teachers, reenactors, museum guides, docents, and other vocations that inform the public about the sum total of what they do (culture) and how they interact with the physical world (environment).

Back in 1984 when I started my first seasonal job as an interpretive ranger with the National Park Service (NPS), I was introduced to a man who would have a major impact on my life. His name is Freeman Tilden and he wrote a book entitled *Interpreting Our Heritage*. Freeman Tilden was a professional journalist who in 1941 was asked by the director of the National Park Service to take on the challenge of touring the National Park System as an administrative assistant and "formulate a plan for public relations and interpretation." (Tilden, 2007, 6) His findings led to the book *The National Parks: What They Mean to You and Me* (1951).

It is funny to think back to when I was in 4th grade and I asked my dad if I could buy a book at a park visitor center. The book I had in my hand was Tilden's *The National Parks*. My father's reaction was "Don't you want something else? Maybe a souvenir?" For some reason I wanted this book!! I don't know why, but to this very day I have treated this book with dignity. It is in the same perfect condition as when my dad bought it for me. Funny how things come into your life!

In 1952 Freeman contacted the NPS to see if they would fund another book. This time he wanted to "get beneath the surface of method and procedure to the underlying principles - to the art and philosophy that should guide efforts to interpret the great scenic and historical heritage of America to her citizens." (Tilden, 2007, 9). The NPS received the grant funds needed, approved his request and he set out to do his research - this time traveling outside of the Park Service to visit Colonial Williamsburg and the Farmer's Museum in Cooperstown, New York. At both places he experienced historic re-creations and reenactments - visitor experiences that he characterized as "animation," or living history. In 1957 *Interpreting Our Heritage* was published for the first time by the University of North Carolina Press.

This book became a foundation block for my understanding the role of an interpreter. When I first received my assigned reading materials for becoming an interpretive ranger at Hopewell Furnace National Historic Site, I quickly scanned Tilden's book. My priorities were centered on iron and only iron! I needed to learn the role of an iron moulder at a charcoal cold blast iron furnace as quickly as I could. Tilden was too philosophical for me so I quickly threw it aside. However, in 1989, when I was nominated for the Freeman Tilden Award (a National Park Service Award given to the best front-line interpreters), I decided to get it out and read it again. Now I pull it out and quote from it on a regular basis. You might say it has become this interpreter's bible of sorts. Many years later my original copy of *Interpreting Our Heritage* is now worn and highlighted and I **retired** it to my office desk - right next to me as I write this book. I even had a retirement ceremony for the event - played taps and all that kind of stuff! But I think you get my gist - it's sort of like having a friend next to me. Yeah, a friend - someone or something that has helped me understand life. And life is personal. Personal…just like living history can become.

My original copy of Tilden provided needed inspiration in the beginning years of my living history career and I will never throw it away. It will always sit next to the Freeman Tilden Award I won in 1989 from the Mid-Atlantic Region of the National Park Service - home where it belongs.

Recently I purchased the 2007 edition of the book and introduced the grandchild to his grandfather. They had a good conversation. The grandchild talked about the new introduction in his edition that lets the reader learn about the personal life of the author. I stepped in and told the grandchild that he would now be traveling with me on a personal basis. Now we travel together to conferences and living history training sessions that I conduct. We go into college classes where I try to inspire my students with Tilden's most important principle – **Love of People**!!!! He said, "If you love the thing you interpret, and love the people who come to enjoy it, you need commit nothing to memory. For, if you love the thing, you not only have taken the pains to understand it to the limit of your capacity, but you also feel its special beauty in the general richness of life's beauty." (Tilden, 2007, 126). He later explained his meaning of love. It went like this:

"Precisely I do not imply any mushy view of humankind, or an exaggerated notion of their virtues…No, indeed; you are not to love people in any sickly sense. You are to love people in the sense that you never cease trying to understand them and to realize that whatever faults they have, whatever levity, whatever ignorance, they are not peculiar. People were not born with the special purpose of making an interpreter uncomfortable…Samuel Taylor Coleridge has explained this to me, who have needed the explanation as much as, and perhaps more than, any: 'If you do not understand a man's ignorance,' said Coleridge, 'you will remain ignorant of his understanding.'…Enough of this aspect of love; and now to the love of his subject that the interpreter must possess. 'To know a thing,' wrote Thomas Carlyle, 'what we can call *knowing*, a man must first *love* the thing, sympathize with it: that is, be virtuously related to it.' Priceless ingredient, indeed." (Tilden, 2007, 127-130).

Tilden's six principles as presented in *Interpreting Our Heritage* (Tilden, 2007, 35) are as follows:

1. Any interpretation that does not somehow relate what is being displayed or described to something within the personality or experience of the visitor will be sterile.

2. Information, as such, is not interpretation. Interpretation is revelation based on information. But they are entirely different things. However, all interpretation includes information.

3. Interpretation is an art, which combines many arts, whether the materials presented are scientific, historical, or architectural. Any art is in some degree teachable.

4. The chief aim of interpretation is not instruction, but provocation.

5. Interpretation should aim to present a whole rather than a part and must address itself to the whole man rather than any phase.

6. Interpretation addressed to children (say, up to the age of twelve) should not be a dilution of the presentations to adults but should follow a fundamentally different approach. To be at its best it will require a separate program.

"Thus the six principles with which I began this book may be after all…a single principle. If this should be so, I feel certain that the single principle must be LOVE [emphasis added]." (Tilden, 2007, 132).

I begin my interpretive methods lectures with this quote. You should see the look on my college students' faces after I tell them that I love them. No, not in some mushy way! But I love you and have taken the pains to understand you to the limit of my capacity. I have learned that when I try to teach about living history I teach about myself. I put me into my teaching and thus embrace it with love in

3

my heart. People who have seen me do living history marvel at my passion for my subject. It is not phony. It comes from within. It is the essence of any good interpreter. It is also the essence of any good actor.

Tilden's definition of interpretation is, "an educational activity which aims to reveal meanings and relationships through the use of original objects, by firsthand experience, or by illustrative media, rather than simply to communicate factual information." (Tilden, 2007, 17). Interpretation is embracing the past in a personal way.

Now it is time to define living history. What is it? I have often wondered about that myself! While performing at various events where I meet other "living dead" people, I have observed different categories of living historians. They include:

1) interpreters/reenactors conducting animations or demonstrations, etc. in period clothing who are portraying a specific historical role - acting as if they were living in the period of the past (e.g., Civil War reenactors who are members portraying life as it was on July 3, 1863 at the Battle of Gettysburg). This is referred to as first person interpretation.

2) interpreters/reenactors dressed in the reproduction clothing representing the past (July 3, 1863) but talking in the language of the present and not utilizing first person role playing. This is referred to as third person interpretation.

3) interpreters/reenactors dressed in reproduction period clothing but representing someone from the past who is on "special assignment" to come back to earth to tell the visitor about the past by speaking in the language of the present. This is referred to as spirit of the past interpretation, or first person past or ghost interpretation (e.g., someone representing Captain John Davis Pawling whose spirit always walks the battlefields of the Civil War in search of people in the present to share his experiences of the past).

4) actors portraying historic figures on stage (e.g., Hal Holbrook as Mark Twain) whose performance often some interaction with the audience while in character.

5) movie actors in a historically themed movie (e.g., Sam Elliot portraying General John Buford in the movie *Gettysburg*).

There are also people employed by museums, parks, recreation areas and wildlife refugees who also, conduct living history presentations as interpreters.

And then there are the "farbs" as they are sometimes called among the more historically accurate interpreters/reenactors. These are the people who take little time to research the past and just wear whatever "old looking clothes" they can find and make up their stories about the past as they go.

Sometimes they have no physical resemblance at all to the character or time period that are portraying (i.e., a grossly overweight Lewis & Clark Corps of Discovery member or someone portraying a character of a totally different race or ethnicity). Many times their lack of research severely blemishes the whole living history community and stains the image and value of living history in the eyes of the "real" historians from the world of academia.

There are also the curatorial folks who often have little time or respect for living history and never want anyone to touch any object considered "historic" without wearing white gloves. This precaution is of great value but sometimes leads to a battle with the interpretive staff over what is an original item and what is a reproduction.

There are also the more structured historians who just feel that living history is an oxymoron. Nothing lives but the present moment, and the present is not yet history. So, why waste your time trying to portray the past inaccurately. According to Marcella Sherfy (*In Touch*, May 1976, 5) -

> "Even having steeped ourselves in the literature of the period, worn its clothes, and slept on its beds, we never shed [present] perspectives and values. And from those perspectives and values, we judge and interpret the past. We simply cannot be another person and know his time as he knew it or value what he valued for his reasons."

Then there is me (a unique blend of interpreter, college professor, living historian, reenactor, naturalist, professional musician, and lover of life) who believes that living history can never reproduce the past in the present but it can wet one's appetite for the past. That is its true value. If we don't know where we have come from (the past), then we can't understand the present. If we can't understand the present, we have no idea where we are going in the future. Again, you can never fully depict all aspects of life in the past by performing living history in the present. It is merely a tool to understand ourselves and where we have come from. We need an understanding of the past for guidance in today's uncertain times. Without any knowledge of the past, we may easily just repeat the mistakes of our forefathers. Living history is one of many ways to explore the past. It is a way of embracing it.

The public supports living history. According to William Alderson and Shirley Low's book entitled *Interpretation of Historic Sites* (1987), "What seems to interest the public the most is people. They are inordinately curious about how people of an earlier era lived, what they ate and wore, what they worked at, what they did for entertainment, how, in short, the lives of the people who were associated with the site compare with the life styles of today."

So let's settle on a definition of living history before we move on into the meat of the topic. My esteemed colleague and good friend Dr. T. Lindsay Baker (the W. K. Gordon Endowed Chair in History at Tarleton State University in Stephenville, Texas) defines living history as "the re-creation of elements of former events or lifestyles as a means of better understanding the past. For many people, living history provides a popular method of more vividly interpreting the past for students or the public." According to T. Lindsay, "Living history serves Dr. Baker as a means to enhance understanding." Amen! Amen!! Amen!!!

Living history is not an end onto itself, but it has opened my eyes to a whole world I never would have discovered had I solely concentrated on only reading history books. Without living history, I never would have embraced the past. How many critics of living history have ever experienced those unique moments when all seems a picture of the past? I must admit they are rare, but at those times something from the past reaches down and makes your view of the past real like never before. It might be something someone has said in the middle of a reenactment or a visual that seems to be taken from the past and it appears in the present. It is eerie.

I do not believe we can ever experience a battle from the past when we are carrying and being fired at by non-bullet loaded firearms. I am certainly not recommending carrying live rounds. As a matter of fact, I condemn that thought entirely. Nevertheless, living history has its value. Being able to work with mules pulling a reproduction canal boat into a canal lock is the activity most representative of actual canal operations of the past as described to me by the late Schuylkill Canal boat captain C. Howard Hiester. It made my interpretation of this event real so that I could teach it in a successful way to my college students learning about the American Industrial Revolution. And, if you cannot grasp my meaning from the first example then here is another that you might understand - especially if you are Pennsylvania Dutch. You can read all about how a good wet-bottom shoofly pie should taste, but, until you dunk a slab of that baby into a cup of coffee, place it in your mouth, and treat your taste buds to that explosion of sensory Nirvana, you do not know wet-bottom shoofly pie. Now that's what good is! Ya gewiss!

CHAPTER ONE

Dr. T. Lindsay Baker and the author explore the Antietam NB (Sharpsburg, MD) on a "Victorian Holiday"

Dr. Baker portrays a Buffalo Skinner.

Rich Pawling (left) and Bucky Green (right) interpreting the French & Indian War period at Somerset Mountain Craft Days (Somerset, PA)

Freeman Tilden – author of *Interpreting Our Heritage* – the "Interpreter's Bible."
(National Park Service photo by M. Woodbridge Williams.)

Above - A view of Schuylkill Navigation Company Lock #43 (Kelly's Lock) near Reading, PA. "If you love the thing you interpret…you have not only taken the pains to understand it…But you also feel it's special beauty" *Freeman Tilden*

Professor Rich Pawling sitting in his office at Hocking College (OH) getting ready to inspire his Interpretive Methods students about Tilden's most important principle – "LOVE."

Using "third person interpretation" to commemorate those who were killed in the 1897 Lattimer Massacre. This union versus management tragedy in the anthracite/hard coal fields of northeast PA gave the author a better understanding of the role of the UMWA (United Mine Workers of America) today. UMWA President Cecil Roberts marches next to the "old miner" (the author) in this 1997 remembrance parade near Hazelton, PA.

Is there something wrong with this picture?

"What seems to interest the public most is people – how people of an earlier era lived, what they ate and wore…how in short the lives of the people who were associated with the site compare to the lifestyles of today." William Alderson and Shirley Low in *Interpretation of Historic Sites*.

According to Dr. T. Lindsay Baker, "living history can be defined as the re-creation of elements of former events or lifestyles as a means of better understanding the past." In this image, Dr. Baker is interpreting the role of an encyclopedia salesman at an event in Beaumont, TX.

Former Schuylkill Navigation Company canal boat captain C. Howard Hiester passes on his knowledge of canal operations in the late 19th to early 20th century to a young enthusiastic interpreter (the author).

CHAPTER TWO

HISTORY MAKES THE LIVING HISTORIAN

Every living historian is a composite of his or her personal history combined with the historical record of the character that he or she is portraying. Your individual personality, developed as an ever-evolving result of your personal background and experiences, **is who you are** and who you are will ultimately be reflected in the character that you represent at any particular point in time. You can never take "you" out of your living history presentations.

Why is it important to know Rich Pawling's personal history before we go any further? Because everything I do and believe in as a living historian is to some degree a product of my personal history. So…on to the growing up years that ultimately led to the totality of this living historian today.

The year was 1951 and the date was Tuesday, March 13. In the Reading Hospital (Reading, Pennsylvania) a blond-haired blue-eyed boy by the name of Richard Nelson Pawling was born to Dr. and Mrs. J. Allen Pawling of Kutztown, Pennsylvania. I would be the new kid in the family of four. My brother Robert was born in 1947. My father, J. Allen Pawling, was a professor of Art Education at Kutztown University for 38 years. My mother, Geneva Leininger Pawling, was a former elementary school teacher who had taught in a one-room school house. In addition to raising "her boys," she excelled at the piano and possessed a passion for Christian music. In fact, before my brother and I were born we were dedicated by our parents to serving Jesus Christ in a family Christian ministry.

When not teaching, my father led the family "on the road," driving a station wagon loaded to the roof with a huge amount of equipment including chalk easel, cornets, music stands, chalks and books. Dad did the preaching and teaching through his "Chalk Talk" ministry. He would illustrate a theme of the church concentrating on Christ's teachings or a hymn (e.g., *The Battle Hymn of the Republic* or *Beside the Still Waters*) or a moral story (e.g., "What is that in Thine Hand," "The People Had a Mind to Work," "The Church is One Foundation," "Keeping Christ in Christmas"). He would speak and then draw in chalk a section of a complete drawing. Then he would speak again and draw again until the entire chalk drawing was completed. Sometimes he drew with fluorescent chalk and, at the end of the presentation, turned on black (ultra violet) lights to make the picture glow in the dark. My favorite all-time chalk talk was his interpretation of the hymn *Beyond the Sunset*. Today memories of my father's words and illustrations still provide comfort when thinking about the impending end of my life and that final journey to go beyond the sunset to be at home with my parents and friends forever more. Before the chalk talk, my brother and I played arrangements of Christian music on our cornets and provided vocal duets as needed. Mother accompanied us on the piano. She also had a beautiful singing voice. Thus, at eight years of age, yours truly was standing before audiences and feeling comfortable doing so. I was beginning to know the feeling of audience approval and I liked it! But that would change.

Although my parents raised us in a home adjacent to the small-town college community of Kutztown, their roots were firmly laid in rural Pennsylvania soil. Their home was in the country at a place called Mohn's Hill. My mother, then Geneva Leininger, was raised on the top of the hill on a Pennsylvania German farmstead roughly ten miles from Reading, Pennsylvania (the home of the same mighty Reading Railroad you may recognize from playing Monopoly!). My father was raised at the bottom of that hill. His father was a foreman for the W.K. Leininger Knitting Mills located in nearby Mohnton.

The area where my parents were raised was settled by the Pennsylvania Dutch. This folk group is not Netherlander Dutch. The name "Dutch" is believed to have resulted from a misspelling or misunderstanding of the word "Deutsche" (which means German) by the English. Thus these German-speaking immigrants were called the Pennsylvania Dutch rather than, more accurately, Pennsylvania Germans. This group of immigrants arrived in Pennsylvania between 1683 and ca. 1800 from German-speaking lands – emigrating primarily from southwestern Germany and especially the Palatinate region (now part of the German federal state of Rheinland-Pfalz). A unique dialect of German, influenced by English, is still spoken by descendants of an estimated 100,000 or so Pennsylvania German immigrants. According to my Pennsylvania Dutch instructor and linguist friend, Butch Reigart –

"Pennsylvania German most resembles the varieties of the German Palatinate dialect ("Pfaelzich") spoken in areas around the German cities of Mannheim and Heidelberg in Baden-Wurttemberg. As of 2009, an estimated 250,000 Americans are still fluent speakers of Pennsylvania German. Most today are Amish and Old Order Mennonites - living in Pennsylvania, Ohio, Indiana and other mid-western states. Perhaps 20,000 or more are Pennsylvanians of "non-plain" background who are affiliated with Lutheran, United Church of Christ or other church groups. The majority of these "fancy Dutch" live in small towns and rural areas of Berks, Lehigh and Lebanon counties and neighboring areas."

Whether visiting my grandfather's farm or playing near the college town of Kutztown, I could not escape the Pennsylvania German influence in my life. My grandparents and my parents would often speak Dutch when they didn't want "the boys" to not know what they were talking about! According to my mother, who was raised on the farm, this dialect was not to be learned by the sons of a college professor. But no matter how she tried to keep the language from us, she spoke words of it in her everyday language. She would say, "stop your rutsching around" (stop squirming); "your hair is schtruwwlich" (unkept); "you are verhuddelt "(confused) or "Oh, the Hawwerlice (oat bugs) are bad this year." Later in life, I heard many a Dutchman say "If you ain't Dutch, you ain't much." No wonder the Irish had a hard time breaking into these German areas. They sure weren't Dutch! Thus "no Irish need apply" (NINA) proved to be true in the Dutch Country.

The "English" influence on my life came from my father's side of the family. My grandmother Emily Pawling lived with our family in Kutztown when I was growing up. The first of the Pawlings to migrate to the New World was Captain Henry Pawling. Believed to be born in Padsbury, England he arrived in New Netherlands (New York) with the Duke of York's army in 1664. On April 18, 1670, he was commissioned at the town hall in Kingston, New York as "captain of the foot company listed and to be listed in the towns of Marbletown and Hurley and Wiltyck at Esopus." He was appointed officer over the Indians at this time, and in 1684 was appointed High Sheriff of Ulster County, serving on many high commissions. On November 3, 1676 he married Neeltje Roosa who immigrated to the colonies from Holland in 1660. For services rendered on behalf of the King and Queen of England he received a land grant in the Marbletown area, ultimately procuring over 10,000 acres in Ulster and Dutchess counties. His lands included the future site of Franklin D. Roosevelt's *Springwood* mansion in Hyde Park, New York. In addition, he had a grant of 1,000 acres in Philadelphia County, Pennsylvania. His sons Henry Jr. and John settled on adjoining tracts of 500 acres at the junction of the Schuylkill River and Perkiomen Creek near Valley Forge (in modern day Montgomery County) – near the future site of the Colonial Army's encampment in 1777. Captain Henry Pawling's library of over 300 books was one of the largest libraries in the colony of New York. The town of Pawling, New York was named in honor of one of his descendants. I will tell you more about the Pawling Family in chapter six entitled "The Character Behind the Characters - What Has Living History Taught Me About Myself."

Once or twice a month my family visited the Leininger Farm where I was introduced to farm animals - up close and personal! My grandparents introduced me to cats, dogs, ducks, Holstein cows and bulls, pigs and chickens. During my unsupervised wanderings on the farm, I discovered other new creatures. In the spring house we caught crayfish (ouch!), frogs and salamanders; then in the pond - snapping turtles, catfish, smallmouth bass and sunfish. Around the farm, we ran into skunks, raccoons, white-tailed deer, and cotton-tailed rabbits. Life was good! Vivid memories include pig feeding time. At four years of age I was barely tall enough to see over the board separating me from the hogs. I would climb up onto the feeding spout and watch as Grandpa dumped in the slop. The sounds of pigs fighting for the slop and the smells of manure and feed filled the air. It was life on the farm and to a small boy, it was entrancing. There was so much to see and not enough time to explore every inch of the farm.

The farm included plenty of opportunities to get in trouble…or get hurt - like when we kids climbed to the top of the silo without anyone knowing we were doing it! Speaking of getting into trouble - I remember the time our grandfather, Elmer Leininger, told my brother and I "to get rid of the rotten tomatoes in the shed." Since he never told us how to get rid of them, we decided to feed them to the cows. Throwing them at the cows, however, was much more fun! We were having the time of our lives "beaning" those cows with rotten tomatoes. They were easy targets at first, but then they took to flight - moving beyond the range of our throwing arms. We quit, thinking all was peaceful and went about our explorations of the farm. Peaceful? Yeah, right! The Great Explosion was coming! When grandpop called his cows in from the field for milking, they came in covered with tomato juice. Oh, did we get a licking! He went for his belt and I can still feel the pain today. He believed in taking the scripture, "spare the rod and spoil the child" literally. We sure weren't spoiled that day! That rod was smoking on our butts. My brother took the worst of it though as I convinced grandpop that he came up with the idea. We learned a valuable lesson from that event, "if you're going to be stupid, then you better be tough" (as was later taught me by my good friend and mentor Scott Kegerise).

Well, when we finally managed to make it into the farm house with our "asses ketchin" grandma Estella Leininger was waiting to hold us in her big arms and comfort our pain. I believe she even had a few words too with Elmer about beating us! I loved her for defending us. She was a real grandmother - the type every child deserves. No tattoos on my grandma! She would have nothing to do with something like that, but would surely say, "That's just dumb!" She was a plump Pennsylvania Dutch woman who could make all those special Pennsylvania Dutch foods: cup cheese, sand tarts, scrapple, shoo fly pies, and pork and sauerkraut, to name a few.

And, she taught us that being raised a true "born again" Christian was the most important thing in life. Even though she was a Sunday School teacher, she had her unique ways and opinions. Living in the 1950s as a Protestant meant disliking Catholics. It was a Republican, Protestant, Prohibition or WASP (White Anglo-Saxon Protestant) thing. As a matter of fact, everyone who attended the church just down the road seemed to have the same dislike for Catholics. One time, when my brother and I were watching John F. Kennedy on grandma's television during his run for President, she told us to turn him off saying, "Nobody in this family will watch the Devil in my home." For years I wondered why she disliked Catholics. When I asked that question at the supper table, I was told that discussion was for another time. "Just eat your food. Children should be seen and not heard at the supper table" was her only response.

It may be said that my grandmother came by her prejudices honestly. While doing genealogical research on the Leininger Family about a year ago, I found an account of one Leininger ancestor who was about to give birth in a Catholic town in what is present day Germany. Though great with child, she walked many miles to a Protestant town so that her child might be spared a Catholic blessing upon its birth.

Living history has taught me that the past has a strong influence on the present. However, new understanding and perspectives and an open mind to what one learns in the present can modify feelings learned in our past. Thank God the dislike for members of the Roman Catholic Church has dissolved in our family. Some of my best friends are Roman Catholics and my brother now substitutes as a teacher at a parochial school. I wonder what grandma would say if she were alive today? "Saag mir eppes neies. Sell is genunk! Was mer net weess, macht eem net heess." (Tell me something new! That is enough! What one doesn't know, doesn't bother one!)

These experiences on the farm were shaping me to become a living historian. How was I to know that someday I would be in charge of the livestock at Hopewell Furnace NHS - which included treating sheep for thrush or hoof rot?

There must be a million stories I could write about what happened on the farm, but there was another place that influenced my life and prepared me for my living history experiences to come. It was the town of Kutztown where I grew up. My dad taught as an art education professor at Kutztown, University of Pennsylvania (previously named Keystone Normal School, then Kutztown State Teachers College, then Kutztown State College). After World War II, houses began to spring up adjacent to Route 222 on what had been farmland for almost two centuries. For twenty-five years I lived along that road in my parents' red brick Cape Cod style home located across the street from and directly in line with the runway from the little Kutztown Airport (which was built after our home was already there). Boy was that fun!! Imagine growing up with small single engine planes coming in for a landing approximately ten feet above the roof of our house and if they miscalculated, as they did on one or two occasions, hitting the telephone pole and electric wires in front of our house and crashing head first into the ground right in our front yard. After a while we could tell if a plane was landing too low by listening to the sound of the engines as the plane approached. Of course we would all run to the window to see if it made it to the runway! Having been born into that environment I never thought it was unusual until my parents had friends and relatives "over to visit" and a plane barely cleared the roof. All kinds of expletives came pouring out of their mouths as everybody went running for cover. Never a dull moment!

As a college professor's son I had the best of both worlds, "the town and the gown." My formal education began with kindergarten at the then college Laboratory School. In fourth grade, I transferred to the Kutztown Public School System and graduated from Kutztown High School. Some of the most wonderful teachers molded my thinking. My high school history teacher, Barry Adams, gets credit for instilling in me a passion for American History. One time he took time from his personal schedule to load a bunch of his disciples in a van and travel to Gettysburg National Battlefield where he gave us a tour of the battlefield worth remembering. We spent the whole day there exploring the battlefield and learning about the past. Today Mr. Adams is a passionate supporter of living history. Thank you very much Barry!

There were other teachers who molded me by way of intimidation - including one of my music teachers who belted me across the face for not playing a cornet solo at the big Christmas Concert. He was some kind of motivator! The auditorium was packed and as I got ready to play the cornet solo (which I played perfectly in practice that morning), I froze on stage and not one note came out of my cornet. I was shaking like a leaf and my mouth was bone dry. Being scared to death that I wouldn't play a perfect solo, what was I to do? I chose the best alternative. I never made a mistake because I never played a note! I just turned around and sat down in the band while my band director glared at me. What a painful experience!

That, however, was a turning point in my life in my performance life. Fear of audiences now flooded into my psyche. I had to fight through it for many years before I could get up in front of large audiences again. Living history helped me overcome that problem. I played the cornet before over 20,000 fans at a Richmond Braves AAA baseball game and never missed one note! Since starting History Alive!^{SM} in 1991, I have conducted over 4,100 interpretive presentations before approximately 850,000 people. My Boys of Base Ball group sang the National Anthem at Doubleday Field in

Cooperstown, NY for the opening of festivities for Cal Ripken, Jr. and Tony Gwinn's induction into the National Baseball Hall of Fame. When professional baseball took over the Grand Ole Opry for its winter meetings, we performed in Opryland and were featured on the home page of the Major League Baseball website. As they say in the world of bull riding, "One day it's the pay window and the next it's arena dust. You got to cowboy up." And, I have a lot in common with those bull riders. I have been riding and slinging a lot of bull ever since I became a living historian. (Just kidding, of course!)

Kutztown was really a great place to grow up. The town had its beginning in 1785 when the first lots were purchased and it was incorporated as a borough on April 7, 1815. As with the rest of Berks County, Kutztown was settled mainly by Germans, most of who came from the Palatinate region of southwest Germany, bordering the Rhine River. The town had a great park that included a Little League baseball diamond. I spent many a day at that diamond believing that someday I would play in the major leagues - the dream of many kids growing up in the 1950s and 1960s. I loved baseball and was fortunate to have had some great coaches who had played baseball professionally in the minor leagues (Max Danner and Lee Trout).

Amazingly, it was through living history that my dream of performing in the major leagues came true! In 2002, the Boys of Base Ball were part of Ozzie Smith's induction into the National Baseball Hall of Fame. And, as previously mentioned, we were again asked to be a part of the induction festivities for Cal Ripkin, Jr. and Tony Gwinn in 2006. Knowing that we would be performing with Ozzie Smith, I asked Dale Petroskey (then the President of the Hall of Fame) if I could get an autograph for my former Little League coach (Lee Trout) who played in the minor leagues for the St. Louis Cardinals and was in poor health at that time. I was hoping to pick up Lee's spirits - honoring him by saying thank you to the coach who got me started loving baseball. Lee had no idea I was doing this. You should have seen the smile on his face when he received an official scorecard from the Hall of Fame with not only Ozzie's signature but also those of Brooks Robinson, Earl Weaver, George Brett, and Ryan Sandburg as well. Again, living history made that moment possible.

Probably one of the most impressionable events that happened during my growing up days was the annual family vacation. Each year during the summer months we loaded up the station wagon and headed out across America in search of natural or historic sites. We visited Mount Rushmore (South Dakota), White Face Mountain (New York), Mount Washington (New Hampshire), Carlsbad Caverns (New Mexico), New Orleans (Louisiana), Boston (Massachusetts), Cheyenne (Wyoming), Montreal and Toronto (Canada), the Great Smoky Mountains and the Blue Ridge Parkway – just to name a few.

The one vacation trip that really made an impression on me was the 1961 excursion that my brother Bob designed. He had a passion for the Civil War and 1961 was the beginning of the Civil War's Centennial. In one great sweeping trip, we visited Chattanooga, Shiloh, Antietam, Vicksburg, Atlanta, Manassas, Petersburg, and Fredericksburg. Wow!!! Of course, at ten years of age playing baseball offered more thrills than looking at cannonballs. Between my mother and me, I don't know who was more bored. Ultimately, mother was willing to modify her attitude towards cannonballs as long as she had enough pretzels to eat. (A true Pennsylvania Dutch woman never "leaves home without a bag.") And, I gradually came around when dad bought me a Union kepi and a toy rifle so that I could shoot at all those imaginary Rebs. As a matter of fact, this trip had a major impact on my future life. I really do not remember if the ranger that inspired me was male or female, black or white. The seed was sown. When my uncle asked me after this trip "what I wanted to be when I grew up?" My answer had changed from an earlier response of being a baseball player. I now wanted to become a park ranger. An interpreter was born.

After my graduation from Kutztown High School in 1969, my parents decided that the Pawling Family Christian ministry would head to Honduras for three summer months on a short term missionary trip. My dad, after consulting with Tommy Skinner of Central American Missions, decided that we should drive to Honduras by following the lesser visited east coast of Mexico – saying we would "get to see the real Mexico" on that route. This trip opened my eyes to a world of different cultures. After fording swollen creeks, being examined by guerilla soldiers, hitting a horse, being spit on, and having suffered under the influence "of Montezuma's revenge," we finally arrived in Guatemala City, Guatemala and received some disturbing news. While filling up the car with gasoline there, we noticed armed jet fighters circling over the city. Upon inquiry as to why they were on alert, we were informed that a war had broken out over the results of a soccer match between El Salvador and Honduras. (Central America does take soccer seriously!) So…our trip to Honduras was officially on hold. If we had been two days earlier in our travels, we would have been in the middle of the warzone. Thank God for guardian angels!

We changed plans and teamed up with two CAM missionaries we met in Guatemala City (Ken Hanna and Phil Blyker) and toured the nation of Guatemala. Remarkably, we even got to see the astronauts land and walk on the moon while visiting a missionary home in the city before leaving "on tour." Dad did his chalk talks, mother played the piano for the brass quartet of Ken Hanna (tuba), Phil Blyker (baritone) my brother Bob (1st cornet) and me (2nd cornet). In one day we traveled from tropical jungles to snowcapped mountains. The trip ended when we got caught in a tropical downpour and our Ambassador station wagon could not ford the raging river. While my brother and father left the car to survey the depth of the river, my mother and I remained inside the car. As the windows steamed up in the tropical heat, we suddenly noticed little hands wiping away the steam on the windows and little eyes looking in at us. I felt like I was in a fish bowl! I don't know who was more shocked to see each other – the Guatemalan children on the outside or mother and me inside the car. What an experience that trip provided. It prepared me for some serious living history events and for overcoming major obstacles when pursuing quality performance.

After surviving the trip to Central America, I entered the world of higher education at Kutztown University. I had no idea what major to choose. My brother majored in history and geography, graduating four years before me. I saw how limited the opportunities of getting a job as a history teacher had become. Because my parents convinced me that I would make a wonderful elementary education principal someday, I majored in elementary education and minored in geography and graduated with a 3.59 quality point average. A few years later I completed the course work for my environmental education certification and the desire to please my parents by becoming an elementary education principal completely vanished.

These were the years when John Denver was singing to my soul. Biology professor Patrick Duddy got me interested in cleaning up the environment. Sam Gundy, my ornithology professor, instilled in me the desire to be a perfectionist. The misspelling of the genus and specie of a bird under observation, even by one letter, meant the answer was incorrect. After viewing movies of America's polluted rivers and seeing the demise of the bald eagle population, the environmental movement became my focus. I got involved with the first Earth Day celebration - handing out seed packets with my friends Woodsy Owl and Smokey the Bear. During my college junior and senior years, I joined the geography fraternity Gamma Theta Upsilon. This fraternity helped fuel my fire for spelunking which was first ignited by my 11th grade Chemistry teacher Barry Sheetz. Today Barry is a Ph.D. professor in Chemistry at Penn State University and we still keep in touch.

Many weekends and spring breaks were spent exploring non-commercial caves in Pennsylvania, Virginia and West Virginia. There were close calls. I once was trapped during a caving expedition when the passage we were exploring became filled with water. Our only alternative was to wade through not knowing how deep the underground river would become. But despite the serious dangers I experienced in West Virginia, John Denver's *Country Roads* became my theme song. I was "young and dumb and full of fun" and West Virginia became my favorite state. In fact, after I married my lovely wife (the former Diane Reinhart) in April 1976, we honeymooned at the foot of Seneca Rocks in a green Datsun pickup truck with an ecology license plate on the front! This is where I had the best meal of my life, spam and beans, while watching rock climbers scrambling up the face of Seneca Rocks. I wanted her to experience one of my favorite spots with me and even shared my warmer sleeping bag with her on a cold evening – true love at its best!

From 1979 to 1981, I worked on my Master of Science degree in Geoenvironmental Sciences and graduated from Shippensburg University of Pennsylvania with a 4.0 quality point average. At the end of my graduate work, Diane and I decided to buy a pop-up camper and camp across the United States on a 9,056 mile trip while I compiled data for one of my graduate research papers. We travelled across Pennsylvania through the Central Plains to the Badlands and Mount Rushmore, up and over the Rockies exploring Yellowstone and the Tetons, then over the Columbia Plateau to the Pacific Ocean at Newport, Oregon on the Pacific coast. From there, we drove south along the Oregon and California coasts, stopped to see the Redwoods and Yosemite National Park, and then drove across the Mohave Desert (with no air conditioning in our truck) and up to the Grand Canyon (where I got altitude sickness), north to Mesa Verde and then south to Carlsbad Caverns. After experiencing the bat flight interpretive presentation at sunset at Carlsbad, we headed east to Dallas, Texas where we took in the State Fair – learning first hand that everything is indeed bigger in Texas! Then we headed north through Arkansas to Mammoth Cave (Kentucky) and enjoyed the fall foliage in West Virginia as we headed back home. We had explored many of America's great treasures. Despite 80,000 miles on the odometer at the start of the expedition, that old 1975 Datsun pickup pulled a Coleman Rebel camper to the Pacific Ocean and back along the same rivers, over the same mountains and across the same deserts that the pioneers, prospectors, speculators and merchants of old had journeyed.

My growing up years were coming to an end and it was time to get employment in the field of parks and recreation and my dream was to become an interpretive park ranger/living historian.

CHAPTER TWO

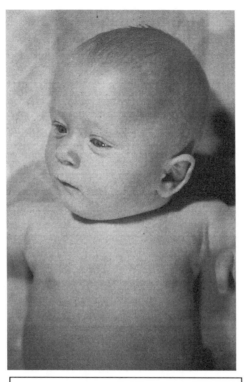

Hello world - an interpreter is born!

Kutztown University where my father Dr. J. Allen Pawling taught for 38 years in the art education department. It was also where my mother, uncle, brother, wife, cousin and I earned our undergraduate degrees and where the author was later named one of the "100 Most Distinguished Alumni of the 20th Century."

Dr. J. Allen Pawling's chalk drawing for his "Battle Hymn of the Republic chalk talk.

Map showing the Palatinate area of the German states – the area from which the majority of the Pennsylvania Germans (often called PA Dutch) emigrated to America.

Making the dust fly at a Pennsylvania Dutch Hoe Down!

Original Pawling grandparents' homestead at the base of Mohn's Hill ("Krick Town").

Grandparents Elmer & Estelle Leininger's farmstead (at the top of Mohn's Hill). Where the author got to "get down and get dirty."

Grandpop Elmer Leininger and his two prized mules. Amazing the way mules were later to become a recurring theme in many of the author's living history programs!

A family trip to the North Lookout at Hawk Mountain Sanctuary (near Kempton, PA) – a special place that had a tremendous influence on my interpretive career. Front row – mother Geneva and grandmother Estelle. Back row – brother Bob and the future naturalist!

Mucking the stalls in the barn at Hopewell Furnace NHS when given the assignment to be in charge of the livestock for a winter. Again, those days on grandpop's farm gave me the experience necessary for the task!

Main Street of the author's home town of Kutztown, PA as it looked in the 1960s.

Pawling home for 25 years of my life - just outside of Kutztown, PA.

Life can be interesting when you live in a home "in line" with a small airport runway! No, that is not "hang gliding" but is a "glider hanging" in the wires.

The Boys of Base Ball working the crowd at a Richmond Braves baseball game.

Having fun on a mechanical bull after performing with the Boys of Baseball at the Winter Meetings of Baseball (hosted by the Texas Rangers at the Ballpark in Arlington, TX). Eat your heart out PBR bull riders!

Dreamin' of making it to the Big Leagues someday! Who'd have guessed my "ticket" was going to be through living history!

My Little League coach Lee Trout cheers me on. Through living history, I later was able to thank him for his efforts.

Who says that your life experiences and the way you are raised do not have an influence your future?? My brother and I on a family vacation.

Exploring the Aztec tombs in Mexico during our 1969 trip to Guatemala.

One of the families in Guatemala who welcomed the Pawling Family in 1969.

Spelunking became my favorite hobby during my college years. (My first date with Diane was to show her cave entrances!) Sure got me prepared for giving underground coal mining tours as Frank Kehoe.

Love that Ecology license plate! Imagine honeymooning in a Datsun pick-up? (The pop-up camper was added later for our cross-country post-grad school adventure!)

Rich & Diane married in a park behind a restored barn on April 10, 1976. (Yes, I'm wearing a polyester leisure suit and Diane's dress is not historically accurate to any period – but what did that matter to us then?)

CHAPTER THREE

OUT STANDING IN A FIELD - EXPERIENCES FROM WORKING IN THE LIVING HISTORY FIELD

Only the totally overconfident (or someone who needs to discover the heights and pitfalls of a profession by "doing it my way") believes there is little or no value in learning from the experiences of veterans in his or her field of vocation. Bear with me as I share some of the challenges and highlights of my thirty plus years in the interpretive field and you may find an abyss or two to avoid in your future (or, if not, you are certain to at least get a laugh or two to make your day!).

My first experience in the field of interpretation was as a naturalist aide with the Pennsylvania State Parks at Nolde Forest Environmental Education Center and it lead to a historian-naturalist position with the Berks County Park and Recreation (BCPR) department. BCPR owns a five-mile stretch of the Union Canal located outside of the city limits of Reading, Pennsylvania. While working for this organization, one of my assignments was to catalog a 5,000 piece canal collection owned by C. Howard and Florence Hiester. The Hiester family were boat builders on the Schuylkill Canal which ran 108 miles from Port Carbon to Philadelphia. Being distantly related to their family, I had a warm relationship with the Hiesters. Howard and Florence treated me like a grandson, and the feeling was mutual.

They donated their collection to the BCPR for the future creation of what is now the C. Howard Hiester Canal Museum. Every time I cataloged an object of the collection, Howard would tell a story to go along with it. I learned from the Hiesters that they loved the past. Matter of fact, they even honeymooned on the Schuylkill Canal on the houseboat Mildred when they got married. (I wonder if Howard shared his sleeping bag with his wife too!) The Hiesters gave me a "soul transplant." Their love of the past (history) became my passion for the present and the future and I wanted to share their stories with everyone who visited the park.

After five years I resigned that position and went on to complete my Master's degree - writing my three Geoenvironmental graduate research papers: 1) *Energy Conservation and Alternative Energy Techniques Employed in National Parks and Recreation Areas of the Rocky Mountain, Western and Southwest Regions,* 2) *Historical Review of Swatara State Park including the Union Canal Feeder* and 3) *An Environmental Land Use Study for the Proposed Williamsport, Maryland C&O Canal Interpretive Center* (funny how my love of canals followed me throughout my career). It was during my masters program that I honed my writing skills which later led to me winning the *Legacy* Magazine Award for Outstanding Feature Article for "For the Love of the Game, Interpreting Baseball" in 2003. I have learned from studying the writings of John Muir, the Father of Interpretation and founder of Yosemite National Park, who said in 1871 "that in order to be a great interpreter, you must be able to observe, **write,** and speak out."

It was with the BCPR (1975-1979) that I made my first attempt at living history since my one-time student teaching experience. Keep in mind these were my first attempts. I always tell my college students that the first attempts are not always the best. I had the passion for the field (my enthusiasm was contagious), but lacked the proper guidance for quality living history. My heart was right to become a living historian, but I needed a mentor to guide me. The clothing we wore was made out of "polyester" and we were to be portraying Revolutionary War soldiers. Ouch! But, the public loved it! We shot guns and cannons, served peanut soup and climbed greased poles and... We were far from historically accurate. Some would say, "Who cares, it's what we instill in the hearts of the public that is most important." I have since learned that **if we instill inaccurate information, we must be held accountable. Ignorance of the past is no excuse for blatant mistakes in the present representing the past.** It is interesting to note that all of this took place during the Bicentennial of the United States in 1976 and there are still people wearing some of those polyester clothes and dresses with zippers at living history events thirty-plus years later! 1976 was one of the greatest years of my life. I got married that year and was also working in the field of interpretation doing what I always wanted to do. Nirvana! But would it last?

In 1973, I filled out my first application to become an employee of the National Park Service. It took me thirteen more years of applications (and fine-tuning my SF-171 with seasonal work) before I finally landed a career position as a park ranger. My first NPS assignment was doing living history at Hopewell Furnace NHS - the most completely reconstructed 18th/19th century charcoal cold-blast iron furnace; some say in the world. What a setting to do my first truly professional attempts at living history! I had always dreamed about doing interpretive living history presentations representing a Union Soldier at Gettysburg National Battlefield at the "High Water Mark." I know I could have described those belt buckles shining in the sun as they did on July 3, 1863, when General Pickett's Confederate soldiers crossed the open field heading for the Union lines. But instead, I got Hopewell Furnace NHS for my first NPS experience. I must admit I knew very little about the iron industry. That was about to change.

Hopewell Furnace taught me that iron was the foundation block upon which the United States was built. Over 500 of these charcoal cold-blast furnaces existed in Pennsylvania at one time. Before we can interpret battles, we must know how and where the firearms and ordinance were produced. Knowledge of iron leads to a knowledge of weapons and he who has the iron conquers the world. England had used much of their mighty forests of oak for the building of its English Armada which ruled the seas. Competing for the felled trees was the iron industry which needed charcoal (made from trees) to produce iron pots, skillets, stoves and other necessities of life. Due to the massive destruction of its forests, England had passed laws as early as 1558 stating "that the felling of trees for the making of coals for the burning of iron was forbidden." England looked to lands across the Atlantic Ocean as a source of wood and iron production. Even though the wooded forests of the colonies compensated for the shortage of wood in England, the Mother Country wanted to control the production of iron cannon and other cast iron products and passed the Iron Act of 1750 which limited the amount of finished iron products that could be manufactured in the colonies. Demanding that the colonies send iron to it in the raw state of pig iron bars, England would then produce the finished products and ship them back to the colonies expecting payment in full. This Iron Act led a number of the signers of the Declaration of Independence who owned iron furnaces or iron rich lands to demand separation from England, which ultimately led to the Revolutionary War because of this mercantilist attitude. Wow, I had never learned that in my school or college history classes!

At Hopewell Furnace, I first started doing quality living history in the third person role as a seasonal. We actually demonstrated the art of flask casting and poured aluminum castings representative of stove plates that were produced at Hopewell during 1836. I learned how to make charcoal and handle horses and I even got dirty (boy, did I ever!). This too is when I learned how to chew tobacco - not demanded but vital when working around charcoal dust. What a seasonal interpretive job I experienced in my early days at Hopewell. Sweating and pouring hot metal 1700 degrees Fahrenheit when working in the cast house; and later chewing tobacco and working with charcoal when portraying George Kephart. Many days I came home looking like a chunk of black charcoal and smelling like a horse with manure clinging to my shoes. In the cast house, we were making moulds by filling flasks with moulder's sand. It was hard work representing the hard times of the past. But we were extremely accurate in our portrayal of the ironmen of the past. I was taught that if we could not prove a fact or representation with three valid reference sources, we could not say it or do it. That first summer I experienced the pain of wearing brogan shoes and the pain of heal spurs! And, many a day my "bones was killin' me." I never needed to waste money to go to the gym after work to pump iron. I was "pumping iron" on the job.

In 1986, I had finally fulfilled my dream by being promoted to career status as a National Park ranger. And, it was at Hopewell Furnace that I got to do first person interpretation for the first time in my career. One day while in uniform and working at the visitor center desk, I overheard two ladies talking about the scene they were observing from the visitor center's windows. The one turned and said to the other, "wouldn't it be wonderful to go back to the past?" My unspoken reaction was, "You have got to be kidding me! In the past, this place was filthy and smoky with horse droppings on the roads. The grass wasn't cut and the buildings were dirty and grimy along with the workers." After hearing that comment, I went to my boss and told him that we were not interpreting the site properly. The lawns were lawnmower-maintained and the buildings were spotless. The steeple-topped cast house which once **was** the iron making center of the community looked like a Protestant camp meeting tabernacle. That is not exactly how the workers of the past described the site when it was in operation from 1771 to 1883! I proposed that since we could not dirty up the environment to look like it would have in the past (because of visitor safety concerns), perhaps I could "hang on the cross as an example of a 1830s ironworker and take upon myself the dirt and the reality of the past" – thus more accurately interpreting that time period without blemishing the site's spotless appearance.

After almost two years of research using the company journals as my primary source of information, I was granted the opportunity of making the past come alive in first person interpretation. The character I chose to interpret held the one occupation that had to be the worst for dirt, dust and filth - the filler of the furnace. Upon consulting the company records, I found the name of a man who was about to change my life forever. His name was George Kephart. Though it might have been more comfortable to take on the role of the ironmaster, Clement Brooke, who owned the site and lived in the mansion in a pristine life of wealth, I chose to portray George. Beyond my original purpose of showing the visitor the true nature of the site's historical past, I wanted to interpret the common laborer who represented 85% of the American public in the 1830's; someone who had little to show in life, lived in a home rented from the company and had a large family to feed on a rather meager salary.

George worked twelve hours a day (6 p.m. to 6 a.m.) for 445 straight days in 1836-1837, earning approximately $16.00 a month. Every half hour he loaded 400 to 500 pounds of ore, 15 bushels of charcoal, and 30 to 40 pounds of limestone into the top of the "fire breathing" furnace and received all the heat and dirt back in his face. It's no wonder the Company records showed that he bought one twist of chewing tobacco for six cents every week in 1836! When portraying George, I emerged from the shadows of the charcoal shed with a bandana over my face and a plug of chew in my cheek. Then I pulled down the bandana and "let 'er rip" with tobacco juice landing in front of the visitors on tour. In the past it was thought that what the handkerchief didn't catch, the tobacco juice would get the rest (the dust, that is). Needless to say, that entrance was an example of provocation at its best!

Anyone who has ever lived near a hard coal miner knows that chewing tobacco and boilermakers (a shot of whiskey placed in a mug of beer and drank in one continuous gulp) were a routine part of that lifestyle. It was thought that the whiskey would loosen the dust in the throat and the beer would wash it down. Remember life expectancy in the 1850s for a man was approximately 35 years of age. Coal miner's asthma or, in the ironworker's world - moulder's lung - would take years off of your life. It's no wonder that the oldest continuous brewery in America, Yuengling Brewery is located in Pottsville, PA in the middle of hard coal and iron furnaces.

My first person living history portrayal of George Kephart got rave reviews from the public. They were beginning to understand that "America's might" was built on "blood, sweat and tears." In 1989 I won the regional Freeman Tilden Award (honoring excellence on the frontline) for the Mid-Atlantic Region of the NPS for this program as well as the admiration of many seasoned interpreters when I presented a small portion of the program at a national conference later that year. (As a tribute to my portrayal of George, the Kephart Family recently invited me to their family reunion. They felt I portrayed George accurately - tobacco and dirt included!) While with the National Park Service I also served on the "Interpretive Skills Team" (teaching up-and-coming interpretive rangers about interpretation and living history) and also was honored to be named to the "Team Resource" training team.

When the year 1991 came around, I left the National Park Service and formed my own company, History Alive!^{SM} – allowing me the flexibility to do living history presentations and training on a more wide-reaching basis. In the past twenty years, I have been able to present living history programs and training in 35 of the United States as well as in Canada. Today, my repertoire of characters includes:

- Christopher "Stoeffel" Stump – 1750s pioneer and friend of Conrad Weiser
- Conrad Weiser - the provincial peacekeeper for Pennsylvania during the French and Indian War period)
- John Jacob Keplinger (Bella Hans) - a Conestoga Wagon wagoner who traveled the turnpikes of Pennsylvania during the late 1700s and early 1800s
- Issachar Pawling who was in actuality my great, great, great, great uncle who worked at Hopewell Furnace in 1836 as an ironworker
- James "Jack" Adair a Pennsylvania ironman who traveled to Missouri and then West on the Oregon and California Trail during the late 1850s
- Levi Bull Smith – 1860s Joanna Furnace ironmaster and abolitionist
- Private John Leininger - a Civil War bugler with the 7th PA Reserve Corps, 36th PA Regiment of Volunteer Infantry, Company H, the Cumberland Guard
- Captain John Hummel - a Schuylkill Canal boat captain of the 1850s to 1870s
- Asa "The Count" Brainard - the feeder (pitcher) for the 1869 Cincinnati Red Stockings Professional Base Ball Club
- Mike Malloy – 1880s railroad "Gandy Dancer"/trackman
- Jack "Grizzly" Hains - a wood hick (logger) working in the logging camps in the 1890s
- Charles Bath "Muley" Tubbs – Oil industry teamster who recalls the oil boom days in PA
- Frank Kehoe - a hard coal (anthracite) miner from 1905 and his bituminous counterpart Mike McKee
- Bucky Jones - 1906 Pennsylvania market hunter and his 1918 Chesapeake Bay waterfowler counterpart, Spittin' Willy Pawley (see below)
- And, the infamous Belsnickel - the Pennsylvania German antithesis of Santa Claus

These characters are the foundation block of my History Alive!^{SM} presentations. Each required hundreds of hours of research.

The Pennsylvania Game Commission (wildlife conservation agency) contacted me in 1993 to consider designing a program for their upcoming 100th Anniversary in 1995. They wanted a stage presentation complete with a log shack stage setting and projected images to tell their story. Working with an exhibit company, I designed a collapsible stage set which provided the backdrop for two characters - Lamar "Bucky" Jones a market hunter from the 1906 period and his present-day grandson John Jones whose father was a game warden. What a story! After doing hundreds of hours of research I found out that the beginning years of the Pennsylvania Game Commission were filled with a great deal of violence. In 1906, there were 14 game wardens in the state and all 14 were shot at, 7 were hit by bullets and 3 died for their service. Bucky was a composite character based on a market hunter who shot a game warden during this time. His grandson was just the opposite of Bucky. He was a teacher who taught environmental education in a public school and reminisced about the changes in attitude that had come about through the past years as they tried to change their family's image.

The show included a rear screen projection unit that illustrated the scenes from the past and the present. During 1995, I presented 220 shows - traveling and performing in all 67 counties in the state of Pennsylvania. That year I ended up doing 361 interpretive presentations and traveling 20,000 miles - mostly by myself. In November 1995, I was honored to receive the "Excellence in Interpretation" Award from the National Association for Interpretation. The Game Commission programs were mainly presented in schools throughout Pennsylvania. For nine months that year, I presented two programs a day (with a different set-up crew at each site) - one for the school students during the day and one in the evening for the general public. Over 70,000 people saw this show and it was a flagship program for the agency. Never before had anyone attempted this kind of demanding itinerary. Believe me; it took total dedication to finish that tour. What a learning experience! Traveling the road can be brutal. Loneliness filled my life. Each day I called a different motel room my home. But my dedication was worth it. To this very day people still remember that show and ask me for my autograph. I also learned what many a traveling band already knows, "One day a hero and the next - a nobody!" The results were worth the ride. In 1996, Maryland's Natural Resource Police hired me to design and present a similar program for their agency's centennial. Then, in 1997, I toured Colorado with a program I created about the wildlife conservation history of their Division of Wildlife. In 1998, the Allegheny National Forest booked me to do a presentation for their 75th anniversary as well.

With the need to expand to new markets in 2001, I designed a four-man interpretive base ball group known as the "Boys of Base Ball" who interpreted baseball's early years (1845 to 1910). Each individual wore authentic uniforms which I designed based on period photographs and paid a seamstress approximately $2,000.00 to reproduce. Who said doing living history is cheap?? If you want an authentic look, then you have to pay the price and "put out the bucks." This group was hired by the National Baseball Hall of Fame (HOF) to interpret the exhibits in the museum including in the sacred Hall of Fame plaque room. In 2001, the manager of the Hall's programs said that we were the first of our kind to perform at the Hall. We have performed there at different events over the years including All-Star Weekend festivities, the National Baseball Hall of Fame Game between the Atlanta Braves and the Minnesota Twins, and were part of the HOF Induction festivities for Ozzie Smith, Cal Ripken, Jr. and Tony Gwinn. At the beginning of a Hall of Fame Game, Bobby Cox, manager of the Atlanta Braves, walked over to me and extended his hand to thank me and my Boys for making the real history of the game come alive. We performed with Brooks Robinson, Earl Weaver, George Brett, Ryan Sandburg, Ozzie Smith, Harmon Killebrew, and Phil Neikro. Thousands of people viewed our representation of "baseball past" during the times we performed in Cooperstown. My greatest thrill, however, was when a small boy and his parents approached me after the Hall of Fame Game and asked if I would autograph his baseball glove. He said that my presentation of Asa "The Count" Brainard was "his favorite part of visiting the Hall of Fame." Who says that the past has no part in the world of major league baseball? The "people in the know" knew that we were providing the best. I even got to go literally nose to nose with the Phillie Phanatic® when he was inducted into the Hall. Imagine the Phanatic trying to shine my bald head! Somehow he did it. I think he used turtle wax and a little elbow grease! And, the head groundskeeper for Doubleday Field thought our way of singing the National Anthem in four-part harmony was the best he had ever heard. My "Boys of Base Ball" have also performed for major and minor league baseball games.

Another thing living history has taught me is that music adds depth to interpretive presentations. I have learned how to play acoustic instruments (mandolin, guitar, dobro, washtub bass, banjolin, lap dulcimer and autoharp) plus harmonica and "things that go bang" because of living history. I had professional training in music when I learned to play trumpet and cornet in public school and college bands but I am totally self-taught on all of my acoustic instruments. These newly-learned musical instruments have opened doors to reach people of all ages and from different cultures. While waiting in the Charlotte, NC Airport Terminal for a connecting flight, I was playing my mandolin in a corner to pass the time. A man from Japan came and sat next to me to listen to my music. Even though we didn't speak a common language, we had the greatest time conversing through music. Now it just doesn't get any better than that! I owe a lot of my musical successes to living history. It has provided the avenue to use music as a form of communication.

Who says living history has no value? Some critics have said that, "all it is good for is to allow overgrown children to play as if they were in the past." What's wrong with never growing up? Could be that some of us living history "dudes" have discovered the "fountain of youth" at last!

CHAPTER THREE

Naturalist Rich Pawling with an osprey mount used in educational programming during my county park days.

Florence and C. Howard Hiester who became like my "adopted" grandparents while Howard gave me a "transfusion" of his love for canals. They honeymooned in the houseboat Mildred on the Schuylkill Canal!

The author's first attempt at living history during
the 1976 Bicentennial was well-intentioned but...

Hopewell Furnace NHS near Birdsboro, PA. An idyllic setting now
for what was historically a filthy, smoky industrial environment.

Demonstrating flask casting with green sand to produce a replica of a 10-plate stove door. Living history can be physically as well as mentally taxing!

Meet George Kephart, the "filler" of the Hopewell Furnace in 1836 – looking cleaner than normal (only a touch of charcoal dust!) in this image. His wife Elizabeth must have washed his clothing prior to this shift! This is the author's first attempt at first person interpretation which led to winning the NPS regional Freeman Tilden award.

1989 NPS Regional Award presentation day with NPS Interpretive Ranger Rich Pawling holding a pen and ink sketch of Freeman Tilden and joined by then Hopewell NHS Superintendent Derrick Cook.

Colleague and friend Jim Cordek portraying Cambria Ironworks owner Daniel J. Morrell with the author as Joanna Furnace ironmaster Levi Bull Smith at a Civil War recruitment rally in Johnstown, PA.

1906 Market Game Hunter Lamar "Bucky" Jones appears on the January 1995 cover of the *Pennsylvania Game News* prior to the 100th Anniversary tour for the Pennsylvania Game Commission. Since the cover image of this publication was routinely a wildlife painting by artist Ned Smith, this one received a wide range of interesting letters to the editor!

"Bucky" Jones in cuffs and leg irons on the PGC float for Ligonier Days in Ligonier, PA. "Bucky" appeared in 220 PGC shows in 1995 – at least two performances in every one of the 67 counties in Pennsylvania!

Maryland Eastern Shore Market Hunter Spittin' Willy Pawley leaning on a battery gun for the 1996 Centennial program of Maryland's Natural Resource Police.

"Dutch" Raymond, the Western market hunter known to shoot elk just for their "ivories" (teeth) in the 100th Anniversary presentation for Colorado's Division of Wildlife. Who says an Easterner can't interpret the history of the West? (Where did the majority of Westerners come from anyway??)

Music is the universal language - adding depth to every type of interpretive programs.

The "Boys of Base Ball" perform on stage along with Tim Wiles at the National Baseball Hall of Fame during Induction weekend for Cal Ripken Jr. and Tony Gwinn.

Is that really the Phillie Phanatic® (mascot for the Philadelphia Phillies) going nose to nose with Asa "the Count" Brainard?

CHAPTER FOUR

GETTING IT DONE:
THE METHOD BEHIND DESIGNING
A LIVING HISTORY CHARACTER

Things to Consider Before You Begin

Reenactors

If you are a reenactor - how long do you want to be involved with this era of interpretation? Many reenactors interpret war periods (e.g., French and Indian War, Revolutionary War, War of 1812, Mexican War, Civil War, Spanish American War, Mexican War, World War I, World War II, the Korean War, the Vietnam Conflict, etc.). And, some reenactors interpret more than one war period. Will the cost to purchase period clothing and accessories make this an affordable hobby?

Employees or Volunteers at a Historic Site

1. If interpreting at an established historic site - first and foremost, **determine if there is even a need for a living history component in the interpretive plan for that site**. And if so –

    *   Is there a research base available to design and support the living history character?

    *   Are there sufficient funds available to support the program? Living history is not cheap if you do it correctly! Reproduction clothing with the proper stitching can be extremely expensive.

    *   Are there long-term interpretive plans and do you have the support of the administration of the site?

- Does the site have the proper personnel who are interested in pursuing this venture and does the site have the time allotted to do this project in an accurate and professional manner? It is my feeling that if you can't do it right, then don't do it at all. Portraying wrong information to the public **just so you can play in the past** for a weekend of partying should be banned.

  - Should we have "**History Police**" who have the authority to stop poorly researched attempts in the living history field? Just as we have black powder regulations inspectors, we need someone to oversee the quality of living history events. But then, maybe many festivals or reenactments would not have any participants. This could get highly political and even ugly, but it's a thought.

  - Should we also test for drug and alcohol abuse before allowing volunteers and reenactors to shoot off guns?

  - And, what about psychological testing three weeks before an event? But then, in reality, how many of Quantrill's Raiders (who operated as outlaws during the Civil War) would have passed these tests? Now, that's worth thinking about!

2. Inventory the potential research sources available to you:
   - Diaries
   - Oral history
   - Newspapers (be careful of accuracy!)
   - Historical atlases / maps
   - Photographs and Illustrations
   - Artifacts from the period
   - Period clothing (museum examples of originals)
   - Period music and songs
   - Church records
   - Tax records
   - Census data
   - Family Bibles
   - Climatological and meteorological records
   - Personal journals
   - Cemetery records
   - Company records
   - Historical Society records
   - Libraries (including special libraries dedicated to industrial history, etc.)
   - National, state and local archives
   - Online data from **authoritative** websites (which may include some of the above)

3. How are you going to portray this character?

- What time frame is to be chosen?

- What setting will be chosen?

- Are there other characters that could potentially evolve from the successes of this endeavor?

- What blend of interpretive techniques are being used to tell the whole story (first person, third person, etc.)?

- Do we need a director to handle managerial problems?

- Have we considered the safety and welfare of the visitors?

- What types of props are needed to set the backdrop? (Keep in mind that these items are not cheap either.)

- How many presentations a day are you planning to do?

- What type of sensitive issues could possibly create visitor dislike for this program? How do you plan to address these issues during or after the presentation? Remember - Civil War General Sherman said, "War is Hell." I ask **you** - how far do we go in telling his story when interpreting the past with all types of family groups in attendance? I know what the politically correct world would do. They would change the past to protect the present.

The PC Dilemma

This is one of the major problems facing living historians. Is it proper to fly the Confederate battle flag in Atlanta for the 150th Anniversary of the War of Northern Aggression? Is it proper to use the N-word when talking about the past in a historically authentic scene? (Listen to the dialogue in the Movie *Glory* where the N-word is used in historic context.) But, try and use that at a reenactment and you might be in big trouble! So, what kind of living history are we portraying? Do we fakelore dialogue? But then, what's wrong with singing "Ho for Louisiana" which happens to be one of the lyrics to the Stephen Foster song *The Glendy Burke*. You all know the N-word has been banned. But what about the phrase "Pecker Wood" used the movie *Matewan* when James Earl Jones representing a black scab wants to slur a white man who has just called him the N-word? Do you see where all this is going? Just the desire to want to shoot the G-word (guns) at reenactments can cause major public outcry – depending on the time and place. What a dilemma!!

To share from a personal experience – after performing at a Boy Scout event, I was accused of using sexual language when, after singing the *Ballad of Jesse James* I explained the history of the James brothers. When I asked for specifics, I was told that I mentioned that they belonged to a gang called the "Bushwhackers." When and where will this all end?

Recently the politically correct crowd wants to rewrite Mark Twain's *Huckleberry Finn*. We, the living history world, sit and do nothing while future generations are being robbed of the truth about the past. If we think the past was, "Oh so beautiful" and that everybody loved each other, we are deceiving ourselves and those we are attempting to educate and inspire. Change only comes when we understand that the good old days weren't perfect! Racism and sexism are wrong, but it's part of our history. We can only positively change attitudes if we understand the mistakes of the past! But how do we go about changing this politically correct pattern which is overtaking our country and the world? The future generations depend on our actions in the present! If no one speaks out for the mistakes of the present, they **will** be repeated in the future!

Who is it that holds the power and has a position of neutrality to make the call on what is said and what is not to be said? The news media? Politicians? Heaven forbid! The public school system where you can't mention religion, Christmas or Easter (all of which happen to be a major component of the Pennsylvania German cultures)? That sounds like discrimination. The PC topic is worth a major written work in itself. Remember that according to Jay Anderson's *Time Machines: The World of Living History* (1984), "many of us living historians have been criticized by scholars as creators of *folkorismos,* a German term for what Americans call "fakelore" - pseudo traditions being passed off as the real thing."

Procedure for Designing a First Person Living History Persona / Program

What are the procedural steps to take to design a specific living history persona/program?

1. Inventory the goals and objectives of the program with the staff. What are the expectations of all of the people involved with this program?

2. Research and read. Start with general information and move towards more specific data.

3. Visit the site with the staff.

4. Get opinions from other proven interpreters as to how they would approach this subject.

5. Compare your plans with the competition (the other historic sites in your area who are already doing first person interpretation).

6. Visit the site alone and let it talk to you. Consider staging issues.

7. Think out the technical issues of performance.

8. Start to design the program using a blend of conflict, interest, fact, and provocation.

9. Acquire the needed period clothing items (see Exhibit 2 for more specific information).

10. Put on the clothes and let the character evolve. Wearing the clothing and performing the character is like an orchestra taking the written music of an orchestra score and turning it into a symphonic masterpiece. Do you feel comfortable with your character?

11. Compare your character to photographs of the past (you should have a definitive resemblance to the people from the past that you are portraying).

12. Give a trial run performance to supportive friends who are willing to be truthful but positive in their support of your beginning efforts and analyze their feedback. Make changes as necessary.

13. Give a trial run performance for select administrative personnel and analyze their feedback. Again, make changes as necessary.

14. Continue to research.

15. Present the program to the public and, again, analyze feedback.

16. Keep researching and make changes where necessary.

17. Maintain consistency of excellence despite doing five presentations a day for five straight days.

18. **Never Stop Researching!** New research can save an interpretive program from continuous boredom.

And also, join a professional organization of fellow living history interpreters and historians. Attend their workshops and learn from your peers.

There are four professional organizations that I recommend –

- ALHFAM - The Association for Living History, Farm and Agricultural Museums

- MOMOCC - Midwest Open Air Museums Coordinating Council (the very active Midwest regional division of ALHFAM)

- AASLH - American Association for State and Local History

- NAI/CILH - the Cultural Interpretation & Living History section of the National Association for Interpretation

Additional Tips for Making a Living History Character Come Alive!

- If you are performing in third person or appearing "out of character" at the beginning of your presentation before going into first person, initiate conversation with the public. There is nothing worse than a living historian who dislikes conversing with the public. I have seen interpreters turn their backs on the visitor or act as if they are working on a project just so they do not have to talk with the public. The whole reason you exist is to share information on the period of history you represent. Be pleasant. Remember that the visitor is not an intrusion into your world or an interruption when you are demonstrating a craft. You are in period clothing to represent the past, not to ignore the public who is in the present.

- During the initial contact, introduce what type of living history you are representing or what type of living history you are about to use. Make sure the visitor understands their role and who you represent historically. If you are in first person when the public approaches, then someone representing the past that is in the clothing of the present (i.e., someone representing the site with a name tag) should set the stage and also guide the public when they ask questions at the end of the presentation.

Asking questions to strangely dressed interpreters can be intimidating to some visitors. Remember that the visitor's questions are a reflection of their past experiences concerning your site or situation and their knowledge of the era of history you represent. We can all name some "stupid" questions that have been asked at living history events such as: Are those rifles real? Were those monuments here during the Battle of Antietam? Did any horses get killed during this battle or was it only the men? Why is that horse's tail beginning to lift up? The visitor brings along preconceived ideas about your site and presentation. Some are correct and some are not. Never laugh at a visitor's "stupid" question! Lord knows, sometimes it's tough! I remember one time at Hopewell Furnace NHS an individual asked me if pig iron bars were fired from cannons. Imagine a bar of iron about five feet long and five inches thick flying across the field during Pickett's Charge at Gettysburg!

- Make the visitor feel comfortable in the living history setting (e.g., if they are elderly, make sure physical needs are met - seating, cool places to rest in the summer time, restroom locations known, etc.).

- Make sure the visitors can see you when you are speaking to a large group and you can see them. If someone is in need of first aid, you need be able to see them. Also, keep your eyes on your props as equipment has been known to walk away at reenactments at the hands of the general public and sometimes event fellow reenactors.

- Avoid looking off into the air when addressing the public. Eye contact is important. Don't talk at the public, converse with them.

- If you are demonstrating a craft such as blacksmithing or handling historic firearms, make sure the visitor's safety comes first (i.e., when using hot metal). It is my personal opinion that the public should never be allowed to handle firearms being used by living history participants/reenactors. Loaded or not, this is not a smart move. A firearm should be respected, not fondled by people who have no idea how to use it. Allowing one person, who has knowledge of how to handle firearms, handle your firearm then presents a problem when the totally clueless wants to hold it next. In that case, you put yourself in the position of having to make a judgment call on who is an authority and who is not. Children of the general public should **never** be allowed to handle firearms. And, when using any firearm (loaded or not loaded) for demonstration purposes, **never ever** point it at the public.

- Don't stereotype the visitor. Try to treat each visitor and his needs individually.

- Not all visitors are interested in your interpretive presentation. Some are very happy to watch and walk on. Do not be offended if some occasionally walk out in the middle of your presentation. If, however, this happens every time, you have a problem that needs to be corrected!

- Be sensitive about the needs of the physically handicapped visitor (blind, hearing impaired, etc.). You would be amazed how many things "blind people" can see. That sounds ridiculous but it is true. Having given many tours for the blind, I discovered that they make more accurate observations about an object given to them to feel than others who could see perfectly. They also use their hearing to compensate for the visual loss.

- Don't talk down or at visitors. Talk with them. Find common ground and go from there.

- Wear you historic reproduction clothing with accuracy. If you are a coal miner coming home from work in the 1880's (before shower houses were made available to the men) then you must be covered with coal dust and your face totally blackened. The way you wear the clothing should mirror your trade. Watch those 21st century intrusions as well (i.e., wrong period eyeglass frames, wrist watches, tattoos or pierced earrings when representing a coal miner in the 1880's doesn't cut it).

- Remember to handle difficult people in a firm but positive manner. You are not being paid (or volunteering) to win arguments with visitors. Share the truth, support it with historical references, but be open to learn from the visitor. Sometimes silence is the best answer. Posture can speak more powerful than words. Who can hate a smile if done seriously?!

- Enthusiasm is contagious. Remember the words of Freeman Tilden - "If you love the thing you interpret, and love the people who come to enjoy it, you need commit nothing to memory." (*Interpreting Our Heritage*). I have found this to be true. When I go into character the facts are no longer outside of me. **They now are me**. It reminds me of a scene from the TV series many years ago, *Kung Fu*. The master teaching the "young grasshopper" (the student) how to prepare for life. "Snatch the pebble from my hand. Only then you have been made ready." That is how an interpreter learns the art.

  Remember one of Freeman Tilden's six principles is that "Interpretation is an art, combining many arts. An art can be taught and successfully learned." We need good mentors to teach the younger generation about our world of living history. While teaching, I always tried to use and mentor interested college students when a History Alive!^{SM} program needed an additional person or two. Many of my "Boys of Base Ball" are former students who occasionally work for History Alive!^{SM} and get paid for the experience.

  When you work with college age men, though, you had better lay down the rules and support the rules with action. Keep in mind that college age men bring along college age problems. Unfortunately drinking, drugs and women have been a cause of some sticky times with some of my players and have led to me kicking some of them out forever. You bend once as a leader and you will break. The image of one loser becomes the image for the whole team. I have worked too hard to get to where I am today. I don't need one mistake to ruin my efforts of many years in the past.

  Being a mentor to young people is very important. If we ever want our living history field to flourish and grow, we must do more than plant the seed. We must hoe the garden making sure the mistakes of living history past do not have fertile ground to grow in the present. This takes time and many times we don't get paid to do it. **But,** consider the loss if we ignore this mission!

- Remember lack of enthusiasm can be just as contagious. If you hate your job as an interpreter, let me be the first to tell you to quit now! This ain't "namby-pamby world." The field doesn't need you. There are plenty of very dedicated interpreters out there who are waiting to fill your spot – "a few good men and a few good women." Now, where have I heard that before?

- Never stop researching and reading (yes, I've said it before, but it's vital!). Research and reading saves a dying presentation.

- Your safety is as important as the visitors. You never know what might happen at your site. On hot days - make sure you have plenty of cold water and ice available. Heat exhaustion is real. I have witnessed a Civil War reenactor die at an event due to heat stroke which led to an aneurism. He died before making it to the hospital. This is not the type of thing you want to witness. You never forget events like that.

- Haste makes waste. Take your time when speaking with visitors. Nervousness can cause you to rush through a program. Remember if this is one of your first attempts, things will improve with practice. Remember Michael Jordan wasn't born with the ability to make every shot. He had to be taught and then he had to practice and practice and practice…

- According to Freeman Tilden "Interpretation must present the complete story and should relate to the whole person." Connect your story and your site to the whole picture.

- Music is the spirit of the soul - even if you can't sing or keep a beat. One of my favorite examples of the use of music is in the movie *Glory* when the members of the 54th Massachusetts know that the next day they will lead the fight; running up the beach heading toward Fort Wagner - totally exposed to cannon and rifle fire. Many are certain they won't live to see another day. But this black regiment wants to prove that black soldiers can fight. The evening before the appointed day with death they gather and sing music and make speeches to build up their strength. What a masterpiece of historical acting. Every time I see that, I am singing along and want to give a speech. It embraces you. You and the past become one.

- Anecdotes and quotes help give the visitor a feel for the past. To quote someone from the past gives the visitor a perspective into the period you are trying to interpret. Quoting the past adds academic support to your presentation. It shows you have taken the time to research and that you have read documents pertaining to the past.

- Humor can break the tension between you and your audience. Too many facts can bore the visitor. A little humor brightens the day. Dirty jokes, though, have no place in programs presented to family audiences. And never, ever laugh at the public. Remember they can return the favor and there are always more of them than you!

- Show and tell interpretation is mindless. What do I mean? Well I am sure you all have been at presentations (especially house tours) where the guide identifies every object in the room. This is the chair the family sat on. No kidding! It is better to tie in the stories of that chair as it was used by mother who would read from a book right before bedtime. Now we have created excitement and interest in the people of the past.

- If you are creating a character that never left behind a diary or journal, then you need to build a timeline of historic data around the period that the person lived. Thus you can talk about things that surely would have been in the news. Remember you are looking specifically for events happening closest to the individual (local) but also don't ignore what is happening on a state, regional, national, or worldwide basis. See Exhibit 1 as an example of a timeline that I developed for a recent training workshop presented to the staff and docents of Booker T.

Washington National Monument. Using a timeline helps give you, the living history persona, a visual of the experiences that would have been influencing your life in the past.

If the individual has written books and journals, you can incorporate quotes into your character. I rarely interpret famous people from the past. For one thing, I never look like anybody who was famous! My preference is to portray someone who knew the famous individual. It takes the stress off of you being an actual person who your audience already "thinks" they know.

- All presentations need themes, goals and objectives. It must have structure. If your program has no goals you'll hit your target every time! A presentation that has no structure just rambles from one subject to the next. You need to write down the outline of your presentation on paper. Every good presentation has a beginning, a body and a conclusion. The key element of your interpretive presentation should be an outline. Don't memorize script. The beauty of a living history interpreter is that they don't memorize script, but they have the freedom to improvise. They connect the interpretive moment to their outline. If a visitor gets you off your plan of action, you can improvise to bring the visitor's inquiry back into your plan.

I like to compare a living history program to the physical body. The outline of a presentation is like the skeleton to the physical body. It gives the presentation form. The facts that we have taken the time to learn are the flesh on the skeleton. And your individual personality gives your character its soul. You make the character come alive! Yes, that can be dangerous.

Don't use your living history character as a forum to voice your personal opinions. The living history character should never provide the avenue for you to make remarks about unimportant or unrelated issues. In other words - get off "of your soapbox." We are to interpret the past. If perchance your opinion and the character's opinion were the same, then "bring it on."

- Every living historian needs to acquire a good **personal library**. Highlight your books. Read them over and over. Let them talk to you.

And also, don't forget the public library (but please don't highlight books borrowed from there!). Bill Gwaltney has taught me "that the key to success is a library card." Use the library - not just the Web! Remember anyone can put anything on the Internet! Be careful what you read. Cross reference and if you cannot find three sources to prove it, then don't say it or do it! Be especially careful with *Wikipedia*. I never allowed this as a reference source for my college students' term papers.

- Don't forget the value of sitting and talking with "older" people. Many folks who are "getting up in years" have a better memory of the past than the present. I am rapidly becoming one of them dudes. Though I hate to admit it, sometimes I find myself wandering around the house trying to remember what I am looking for (certainly some you can identify)! But really, the elders in our society should not be "put away" when their minds are still flawless about the past. Yes, it takes time to sit down and converse with them. Take a recording device along (if they allow it) and record their answers to your questions. Be prepared, making sure you have a list of questions that you want to ask or else this conversation could wander endlessly around in circles. That's called oral history. Remember also that not everything they say one day may be stated the same on the next. Be careful of mistakes. Also, remember that some folks will make up things so that their unimportant past becomes more exciting. We all wish we were someone else.

- **Above all, enjoy yourself. Body language speaks louder than words.**

CHAPTER FOUR

Period photographs (when available for your character's time period) are a great source of both clothing, hairstyle and even sometimes mannerisms. Though original period clothing should never be worn, it is an ideal primary source when designing reproduction clothing or selecting the suitable patterns.

One of our rare finds at a local antique market – a period tintype of men in working class attire (at least the two seated).

The Belsnickel is an example of a first person program that requires an advance 'set-up" or explanation by another costumed or non-costumed interpreter. This somewhat scary 19th century character visited Pennsylvania German homes on Christmas Eve (often at the invitation of the parents!) to reward the good children and punish the bad before St. Nicholas arrived on Christmas Day bearing gifts.

It is important to wear the period clothing and practice mannerisms and poises before the actual program. Here the author is getting to know his character, "Stoeffel" Stump, friend of PA's provincial peacekeeper Conrad Weiser prior to and during the F&I War period (1754-1764).

Canal Captain John A. Hummel talks to visitors at the C&O Canal NHP in Great Fall, MD prior to the departure of a canal boat ride.

First rule of using a firearm (loaded or not) – **Never, ever point it at anyone!** And…even if pointing off to the side, be certain that is not where the newspaper photographer is standing!

GONE...

BUT
NOT
FORGOTTEN!

This cover of a History Alive! brochure contrasted the actual coal miner (top) and the author's living history "look" representing the past. *(Upper photo used by permission of the PHMC Bureau of Historic Sites & Museums / Anthracite Museum Complex in Scranton, PA. Ferrotype of R. Pawling by Scully & Osterman of Rochester, NY.)*

Mentoring requires both a seasoned veteran interpreter and a "young buck or lass" with the true desire to learn. Here the author shows Dan Riegel some interpretive "passion." *Photo by Austin Dam Memorial Association.*

Dr. T. Lindsay & Julie Baker have been true mentors to Diane and I over the years since we met through mutual friend Bill Gwaltney.

Education doesn't always come from schools of higher education. It comes from the heart! From one old hayshaker to another – thanks Freddy for being my teacher.

Go ahead and make my day! Try mentoring Penn State Berks ice hockey players as a volunteer academic advisor. Years later many of these guys still keep in touch to talk about those "memorable moments."

Cornet bands were popular during the late 19th and early 20th centuries. If you play the cornet and are interpreting those time periods, "blow your own horn!" *Photo by Austin Dam Memorial Association.*

Buglers during the Civil War were extremely important in relaying commands from the officers in command to the infantry.

Wood Hick Jack "Griz" Hains kicks up his heels. Remember – enthusiasm is contagious!

CHAPTER FIVE

IT TAKES ALL TYPES:
THE PEOPLE WHO I HAVE MET IN LIVING HISTORY

When you are ready to find employment in this field realize that all is not a bed of roses. The field of living history/interpretation as an occupation is not all play and having fun. Realize, too, it's a very competitive world out there – a world where not everybody loves and supports one another though I wish that wasn't the reality. Do you know any field of employment that is perfect?

Having worked in the field of living history for over thirty years, I have witnessed the good, the bad, and the ugly. Though the positive greatly outweighs the negative, I don't want to paint a picture that all living historians/reenactors and folks working in the supposedly idyllic world of parks and museums are always of sound judgment. I want to be realistic. I have served under administrators who had no people skills and were extremely incompetent as managers. Some should have never been allowed to supervise another human being. Under one command, I witnessed an employee take his life. Having confronted the boss as to how we could have helped to prevent this tragedy from happening, his response to my inquiry was that the individual who took his life "was a loser." Wow! Now wasn't that a statement of anything but love and concern in a time of tragedy? In my estimation the only loser was the boss...and I proceeded to tell him that. Well, I guess you might say I won the battle that day but lost the war as I resigned from that position a number of months later due to burnout. As a favorite song of mine (*The Gambler* made famous by Kenny Rogers) suggests, "you got to know when to hold'em, know when to fold'em, know when to walk away, know when to run." Life is too short to "gut it out" in an unbearable situation. There is no shame when you walk away to fight again another day.

In another situation, I had a boss who wore camouflage and hid in the bushes to evaluate my interpretive tours! In one instance, a visitor saw this bizarre behavior and brought it to my attention. I told him not to worry - that he (the man in the bushes) was merely my boss who was evaluating my presentation! I have observed fist fights between administrators and employees and I have been physically threatened – all in the generally perceived "peaceful, quiet world" of park interpretation.

On one hot, steamy summer day after trying to survive five scheduled presentations a day that included horses in the hot sun, I was threatened by a fellow employee in charge of a team of horses who said he would run me over if I didn't hold his horses immediately. Considering that his horses didn't seem to need holding and that he was not my boss, I decided to continue doing my job – communicating with the public. But that wasn't good enough for this individual. He started yelling at me in an angry and loud voice. He then threatened to run me over with his horses. You might say that a scene from the "O.K. Corral" was about to take place. The next thing you know I shouted back at him and told him that if he tried to run me over, I would impale him with my pitchfork. This whole scene took place with park visitors watching the drama unfold. In fact, one visitor later remarked to the uniformed ranger that was leading the tour that this was one of the best examples of acting he had ever seen! The fight was not an act. The situation got out of hand and although we both later forgave each other, the memory still lingers.

Then there was the boss who disliked interpretation but was in charge of the interpretive programming. This individual referred to interpreters as "yogurt suckers, fern feelers, tree huggers, and worm wigglers." Now, he sure knew how to motivate his employees! Of course, he was a real "law dog" who carried a pistol. One time he demanded that I remove a hornets' nest by using a broom handle and "bee spray." I told him I wouldn't do that because there was a safer way to eradicate the insurgents. He called my response insubordination and threatened charges. Well, while I was working at the visitor's center desk the next day, dressed in uniform, a child approached the desk and handed me a couple of live rounds of ammunition from a police firearm. He told me he found them near a hornets' nest that had been partially destroyed. The light went on! It appeared that my "tough" boss tried to knock down the nest with a broom handle and a bottle of bee spray and in the process the hornets attacked him and, while trying to swat them away, he hit his cartridge box and the "live" ammo flew in all directions. What an embarrassing scene (not to mention dangerous) when visitors found the rounds the next day!

The one good thing that I learned from this situation is that I will never take that kind of intimidation from anyone ever again. Some of my "tough" characters (e.g., the logger, ironworker and market game hunter) portray an attitude that I learned while working under a tough individual. It's funny how the past (the good, the bad, and the ugly) have worked their way into my personality. How much influence does the character you portray have on your "normal" life (and vice versa as mentioned before)? Think about that.

There have been times when driving alone in my car that I start to talk to myself as one of my characters. It gets real interesting when two of my characters start to argue with each other! That happened while driving in Ohio. Sometimes it's more than one character that emerges. There I was driving in my Ford Escape SUV when market hunter Bucky Jones, Pennsylvania Dutch canal captain (Cappy Hummel) and the GPS "woman" started to argue about which was the best route to take to a performance site. I had to get in the middle of the fight and tell them to "knock it off" or they wouldn't get ice cream before going to bed that evening. At least I could turn off the GPS woman. The other two kept arguing. Good thing no one else was there to hear that one!

Then there was the time I rented a home in an "Appalachian red-neck area" (home to Meth Heads and Moonshine Monkies) while teaching in southeast Ohio. Having learned (after signing the lease) that a neighbor had blown his house to "kingdom come" while making meth, I wasn't feeling too sociable. Then one night some "hillbilly dude" was pounding on the **side** of my house. I approached him with a 45 caliber pistol tucked in my pants. And, voila, Bucky Jones (the market hunter) appeared inside me. It seems Bucky spoke his language and being able to spit a stream of tobacco juice within an inch of a tough guy's feet had a way of stopping him in his tracks. Then I put on my market hunter stare and talked in the same accent as the dude I was confronting (with the rest coming naturally). My "Dutch" came out and it got real interesting! Well, needless to say, I never saw that dude again! You might say that he became history. I have been told by a Native American associate that "crazy white man is big medicine." You know, he may be right!

Speaking of crazy living history reenactors - I know of a situation where a living historian decided to shoot live ammunition over the heads of the enemy reenactors while having a fake gunfight. He happened to hit one of the "enemy" and that individual is now paralyzed from the waist down for the rest of his life. You wonder why living history has a bad reputation among certain individuals. We have earned it!

Well, that's enough for the bad experiences. In my travels through life, I have met many people who did not work in the living history field but who have molded my life and can be found in many of my characterizations of people from the past; along with fellow interpreters/living historians who helped to create me as I am today. Remember that your personality is a major part of the persona of the person from the past who you represent. You become your character and the character becomes you. However, as much as you think you become the past, you can never shed present day influences upon you character.

Who I am is a direct result of the individuals who helped make me:

Diane Reinhart Pawling--my wife and "God Bless her soul." She has seen me "through all the changes in our life" (a quote from our self-authored wedding vows). After 35 years of marriage she has been there through the thick and the thin. No one has influenced my life more than she has. She has allowed me to reach for my dream and thus many times has been the economic support behind all of those lean years. If you are going to try and make living history your occupation as a private interpretive consultant you better have a cast iron foundation block to stand on.

Dr. John Allen Pawling and Geneva Leininger Pawling--my parents definitely were the center of my upbringing and their influences on my desires to do living history have been paramount. Although I might not have turned out to be what they imagined, I would become, according to Dr. Jack Grossman (one of my father's fellow art education professors) someone "they would be proud of." I can't wait to spend time with them again someday discussing all that they missed about my life while at a distance during their absence on earth.

Robert Pawling (my brother)--he too has had a great influence on my thinking and was my inspiration for loving history and also finding a relationship with Jesus Christ. Although many people think that we can't possibly be related, because we are sometimes total opposites, the bond between us is strong. We have learned through the forgiving love of Jesus Christ that we can except each other's failures and successes. He now is a retired history teacher and travels extensively all over the world sharing the gospel of Jesus Christ.

My Labrador Retriever dogs over the past two decades (Warm Brandy, Saltwater Taffy, Little Zaccheus, Courtney Jean, Chunk of Coal, and Log Cabin Little Princess Perky). Some people would think I have lost my mind for including dogs as having an influence on my living history career, but it is true. I have a bumper sticker on my mandolin case that sums up the status of my dogs. It always brings a reaction when people read it. It states, "The more people I meet, the more I like my dogs." I have never met anything on this planet that shows "unconditional love" like a dog. I have often said that dog spelled backwards is God. I had a Native American associate who said that calling God a dog was an insult, because his nation ate dogs. Well, try and cook up one of my dogs and you will meet the wrath of God! These critters have taken me through some of the darkest moments of my life. Their support has sometimes made the difference between quitting and moving on.

Bill Gwaltney--a brother not by birth, but still a brother. No one has had a bigger impact on my living history impressions than this man. Now Assistant Regional Director for the Rocky Mountain Region of the National Park Service he was involved with putting together the 54th Massachusetts Regiment for the movie *Glory*. I first met him at a National Association for Interpretation Workshop in St. Paul, Minnesota where we were both regional Freeman Tilden Award winners. We were backstage at a banquet which was designed to showcase interpreters who did "costumed interpretive presentations." There were naturalists costumed as trees, bats, butterflies, sunflowers and standing next to them were living history characters representing voyageurs, mountain men, a Bent's Fort fur trader (Bill Gwaltney) and myself as George Kephart (the filler of a charcoal cold-blast iron furnace). I was covered with dirt with my cheek bulging with tobacco. (It amused me to think that Mr. Tree should have been running scared of me for I should have been making him into charcoal to throw into the fiery furnace but we all stayed civil.) I remember Bill coming up to me, offering me his business card as a fur trader, as I told him to keep it because I couldn't read or write. I then proceeded to spit a lake of tobacco juice into my tin cup. Well it was brotherhood at first fight (ha!). Neither of us won the national Freeman Tilden Award, but I will tell you we sure have stayed dedicated to the living history field and have made a difference. Sometimes **not** winning the "Big Award" doesn't mean you won't make a difference. It has been said that real winners never quit and losers never win.

When I later saw Bill at the conference, he told me to do my family genealogy. He wondered if there might be a black branch on the Pawling family tree. He was representing the African-American race and I look 100% Caucasian. I remember laughing to myself when we parted and saying to myself – "no black blood in my family." But guess what! He was right. I found that the Pawling Family does have a black line. (More on that subject in Chapter 6 - The Character Behind the Characters: What Living History has Taught Me About Myself.) Bill is also a proud father and is passing on his love of living history to his son Will who recently spent a summer at the U.S.S. Arizona Memorial (Pearl Harbor, Hawaii) as a volunteer interpretive ranger.

Daniel Esh - an active member of the Amish Community who has allowed me to fellowship with him and his family. After finishing a presentation on the "100 Years of Wildlife Management in Pennsylvania" in 1995, I got to meet some members of the Amish comunity who were in attendance at a show in Lancaster County, Pennsylvania. They stayed behind to talk to me after the program and wanted me to know that they liked the show because it taught family values. A few weeks later I was invited to do a special performance of this show for the Amish Community at the Bird in Hand Fire Company building. I was told they would come and see my presentation after they were done milking the cows! The Pennsylvania Game Commission agreed to let me add this performance to my contract. I was told this was the first time they were contacted by the Amish in the history of the agency. I met with my crew for the evening and we set up the replica log cabin for the show and then looked outside to see if we had any takers. The parking lot was empty! I asked myself, " were they going to show up or not?" Some of the Wildlife Conservation Officers (WCOs) in attendance were baffled as well. About 30 minutes later I looked out the door and there stood over 50 Amish families waiting in the parking lot with their horses and buggies. I told one of the WCOs to invite them in and they in turn asked me to go out and speak a little Pennsylvania Dutch with them and break the ice. It worked like a charm as one by one they filed in. Kids sat up front with the women on one side of the aisle and the men on the other (just like they were having church). It was one of the most fulfilling moments of the whole tour (220 performances). When it ended I shook everybody's hand as they left the auditorium. The male Amish loved it. Some of the women just smiled.

I later met Daniel Esh through my best friend Ron Fink who happened to buy one of Daniel's beautiful wood carvings at an Amish sale. When Daniel later introduced me to some of his family, they remembered me as Bucky Jones, the star of the show! Their hearts warmed to me. Thanks to Daniel Esh and living history, my eyes were opened to understanding people from a different culture. The world needs more people like Daniel. I now have a deeper respect for the Amish and what they believe.

(See the acknowledgments for a continued listing of people who have "made a difference in my life.")

Life is a journey and the only way you will survive is to concentrate on the positive. And, believe me, that's not easy! You have to live with the good, the bad and the ugly moments and remember that tough situations build character within you. The best interpreters are the ones that have made it through the hard economic times and still have a desire to share their knowledge about the past. I encourage you to never give up.

Below is an anonymous poem that was shared with me by the superintendent at a park where I was working when a difficult situation arose. I hope it encourages you as it did me - to set your sights on the horizon and keep marching on.

DON'T QUIT

When things go wrong, as they sometimes will,
When the road you're trudging seems all uphill,
When the funds are low and the debts are high
And you want to smile but you have to sigh,
When care is pressing you down a bit -
Rest, if you must, but don't you quit.

Life is queer with its twists and turns,
As every one of us sometimes learns,
And many a fellow turns about
When he might have won, had he stuck it out.
Don't give up though the pace seems slow -
You might succeed with another blow.

Often the goal is nearer than,
It seems to a faint and faltering man,
Often the struggler has given up,
When he might have captured the victor's cup;
And he learned too late when the night slipped down
How close he was to the golden crown.

Success is failure turned inside out -
The silver tint of the clouds of doubt,
And you never can tell how close you are,
It may be near when it seems so far,
So stick to the fight when you're hardest hit:
It's when things seem worst that you mustn't quit!
Author Unknown

I was reminded at a funeral of a close friend who died very young in life that "the Bible never tells us to win the race, but just to finish the race." Amen!

CHAPTER FIVE

Would you pound on the side of a house if you knew this dude lived there??

Rich & Diane Pawling portraying Levi Bull Smith and Emily Badger Smith – the ironmaster of Joanna Furnace (near Morgantown, PA) and his wife.

My brother Bob "going flying" in a WWII Texan aircraft. His lifelong love of flying was the product of being raised in a home next to the Kutztown Airport.

The four-legged companions who have helped me to continue on in the toughest of times...

My first dog - Warm Brandy. The "God Mother" of Log Cabin Kennel.

Top to bottom above – Lil' Zac, Courtney Jean and mother Saltwater Taffy (granddaughter of Warm Brandy).

My "Canal Dog" Chunk O' Coal.

As we were picking out our next "adopted child," which one do you think won our hearts? Of course, the one posing in the middle - Lil' Princess Perky.

Bill Gwaltney as Ibrahima (the West African Prince sold into slavery) and the author as his owner Thomas Foster performing in the two-person play "Prince of Slaves" at the Natchez (Mississippi) Literary Festival (1994). The play was co-authored by Bill and Dr. T. Lindsay Baker and was based on the book *Prince Among Slaves* by Terry Alford – a "must read" for every living historian.

CHAPTER SIX

THE CHARACTER BEHIND THE CHARACTERS:
WHAT LIVING HISTORY HAS TAUGHT ME ABOUT MYSELF

Many times living historians have been looked down on in disdain by academicians who find no educational value in this technique of interpreting the past. They believe that in order to do living history all you need to do is find some old clothes, use your imagination and portray the past using Hollywood movies and television as the source of so-called truth. As we all know, movies are usually (except in rare instances) the worst source of accurate information about the past. Another often inaccurate source is historical fiction novels. The background for this genre is historical, but the authors often take great liberties in portraying the truth. There are, of course, exceptions where historical novelists (e.g., James Michener and Allan Eckert) have thoroughly researched their topic and strive to present a historically accurate setting for their fictional characters.

Also, we need to consider that just the topic of history has many sides to the tales that are told. Whose history is it? The victors or the so-called losers? The strong or the weak? Which side of the story are you going to choose to interpret?

Despite all the negative commentary about living history, it does have many positive qualities. When I first started to get involved with the field and began to do serious research on my characters, I kept running into relatives from my family's past who were associated with Daniel Boone and George Washington, were captured by Indians at the Penn's Creek Massacre, owned property adjacent to Valley Forge, worked at Hopewell Furnace as iron workers, served during the Civil War as a captain in the PA 68th Volunteers 4th Regiment, Company I and died at the Battle of Chancellorsville, and built equipment that went north to Alaska in search of gold. And, mentioned in a previous chapter, I found a black line in my family that I never knew existed. It seems that wherever I traveled or whichever character I was researching, I found one of my ancestors. You might say I found myself! This blew me away! I never thought that my lineage had any value to the totality of American History. And, it didn't stop there. We (my brother and I and other genealogists in the family) connected our family lineage to Germany (the Leininger side of the family) and to England (the Pawling side). You might say that I was a part of the past before I became the past (as a living historian)! Shocking at first, but why was I so ignorant of this fact? That is what all of us should be discovering as we research our genealogy.

You may just discover that your family is a very important part of America's heritage. **History is People!**

History is People!® became the slogan that my company has trademarked for our videos and musical recordings because I want to let the world know that history is not merely dry facts in a textbook, but has heart and soul and breath. The world of the 18th, 19th and early 20th centuries (which I represent in living history) wasn't nearly as populated as our world is today. Fewer people means that there are more possibilities of connections between one person and another of the same generation and geographic area. Keep in mind that not everybody lived in the upper crust of society. One side of the Pawling Family had wealth but the rest represent the very people I portray today - the nobodies; the common workers who were the backbone of America. The Pawling side went to fight in the Civil War and the Leininger side paid to send someone to fight in their place so they could work the farm and feed the soldiers. Each side of the family had their own views. However, there were also similarities such as being Republican and Protestant (the political and religious views of both families). I have often wondered if we inherit any of these qualities/beliefs when we are born? Is there a possibility that because my relatives of the past worked in coal mines, I would inherit the "no fear" attitude of crawling around in caves during my high school and college years? My parents certainly never encouraged my spelunking adventures, but I guess they decided it was safer than allowing me to join a motorcycle gang! In other words – is it possible that we inherit connections to previous occupations and interests from our ancestors in the past? I know that sounds ridiculous, but I believe some of you who are involved in living history have also found the same mystery to be true. Maybe it's a coincidence. But, maybe it's not!

In Chapter 5, I mentioned Bill Gwaltney and his influence on my life. His challenge to me when we parted at the NAI National Conference in St. Paul, MN in 1989 was to do my genealogy; believing that I might have a black line in my family. Bill is of the African-American race and I thought I was of the Caucasian race only, but little did I realize that I was in for a great awakening. When my father, Dr. J. Allen Pawling, taught in the art department at Kutztown State College (now Kutztown University of Pennsylvania), there was another professor named Dr. John W. Pawling who was an African-American who taught in the Geography Department. Although the two professors casually conversed at faculty functions, neither felt that they were related. In those younger days of my life, I didn't have the time or the desire to search for the truth. I was a college student with a ton of other more important issues to think about (looking for girls, trying to be cool, etc.).

When I landed my career NPS interpretive position at Hopewell Furnace NHS, I was doing research for my living history character, George Kephart. And, that is where my journey for trying to find out who I am really began. While reading the company journals the names of Pawling, Paulin, Pauling, Paulding, Powling, appeared in the company payroll records. They were all associated with the same family. In the era prior to computers and databases, the spelling of a surname often varied according to how it sounded to the compiler of the handwritten records. And, depending if the man's mouth was full of tobacco (a Pawling tradition) when saying his name, it could have resulted in the many varieties of the name Pawling in the journal. (Just kidding!) Other reasons for the misspelling of the name include bad penmanship that was incorrectly copied by someone else at a later date. It is a fact that my great, great, great, great uncle Issachar Pawling did work at Hopewell Furnace. All of a sudden, I had a personal connection to my research on the iron industry. My research was no longer some laborious boring assignment. I was learning about myself (the Pawling Family). You might say I had come home to my past. Now I was anxious to learn more and to continue to research.

While conversing with NPS rangers stationed at Valley Forge National Historic Park, I found out that the Pawling name appears often in the area surrounding the park (Pawling's Baptist Church, Pawling's Mill, Pawling's Bridge, Pawling's Schuylkill Canal Lock, Pawling's Road, Pawling's P.O., etc.). And bingo, I discovered another connection to my family! I found out that, Henry Pawling (son of Captain Henry Pawling) left New York in 1719 and moved to Pennsylvania settling on a tract of 500 acres at the confluence of the Schuylkill River and Perkiomen Creek across from Valley Forge.

Some of the Pawling Family stayed in New York. Major John Pawling (1732-1819) served in both the French & Indian War and American Revolutionary War. He built Pawling Manor north of Rhinebeck, New York in 1761 where he later entertained General George Washington. One of his children joined the Moravians in 1742, becoming a missionary to the Indians in Pennsylvania and Ohio and in 1746, married a converted Indian woman. They had two children, one of whom (a son) was murdered by white settlers.

The Rhinebeck area of New York just happens to be where one of my living history characters (Conrad Weiser) lived after emigrating from the Palatinate area of present day Germany. An adopted Mohawk Indian, Weiser became Pennsylvania's Provincial Peacekeeper from 1731 until 1755. He helped establish Berks County (Pennsylvania) in 1752 and it was a Pawling Family member (another Henry) who carried the approved petition establishing Berks County to the Governor of the Commonwealth of Pennsylvania. Wow! I would never have known these facts if it was not for my living history research. And the connections go on and on and on…

While researching the lineage of Daniel Boone for the visitor center introductory video presentation for Daniel Boone Homestead (in which I was the principal actor representing John DeTurk who owned the Boone House where Daniel was born and visited in 1788), I found out that the Pawling Family knew Boone as well. Daniel Boone served as a wagoner (teamster) on the Braddock Expedition which was given the task of removing the French from the Ohio River Valley. When General Edward Braddock was defeated and killed on July 9, 1755, at the Battle of the Monongahela, the retreating British regiments under Colonel Dunbar encamped at Pawling's Tavern (near Mercersburg in Franklin County, Pennsylvania) from August 4 through August 13, 1755. George Washington was also on that expedition. And then, to really bring our family history to life, I was asked a few years ago to perform in the area of Pawling's Tavern for a historical festival concentrating on the Pawling Family during the French & Indian War.

While traveling across the state for the Pennsylvania Game Commission tour in 1995, I met a teacher in Clearfield County – another Pawling. While conversing, he asked me if I ever attended the Pawling Family reunion in Washington, DC? I told him I had never heard of that one. Well, he went on to tell me that his brother and he went to the reunion and got quite a surprise. When they opened the door to enter the event, they found that all the other Pawlings in attendance at the reunion were African-American. Wow!! As soon as I heard that news, the wheels inside my brain started to turn back to Bill Gwaltney's marching orders to me in 1989 – "check out your genealogy, you might just have a black line in your family." And, you know he was right! But, where did this branch originate since all Pawlings in America trace their roots back to Captain Henry Pawling of New York? The most likely connection is from one of the Pawlings who were slaveowners in the 18th century. My research has uncovered numerous accounts of the Pawling Family owning slaves. As listed in his will, John Pawling of Philadelphia County, Pennsylvania had six slaves in his ownership in 1733. But it didn't stop there. The census records of 1790 for Franklin County, Pennsylvania show that Hendrey (Henry) Pawling owned the most slaves in the county – a total of eight. Knowing that information, I now wonder whether my great great grandfather who died in 1863 at the Battle of Chancellorsville was fighting for the preservation of the Union or the eradication of slavery? A good question! How did the black name enter the family? Was it through sexual/blood relationships or by a common practice where former slaves (having only a first name) accepted the surname of their owner upon release form bondage?

One more time I sat without any answers to my questions. All I know at this point in time is that I couldn't wait to call Bill Gwaltney and tell him that he had "another Bro in the family." I share this story with everyone that I meet. Some black folks have embraced me as a family member and others have referred to me as a "white N-word lover." Well, imagine that! Racism can be found on both sides of the line! But, let me tell you - I am proud of my black heritage and Bill knows that. We have talked about it at length and it has led to a closer bond than we had when we first met in St. Paul.

Sure, "all I wanted to do was wear old clothing and go back to the past." But now the past has liberated me to the freedom of knowing who I am. I wish all Americans could come to that understanding! It was the dream of Dr. Martin Luther King, Jr. to have "black and white working together." That is my dream as well.

While researching the history of Conrad Weiser for my portrayal of him, I found another connection to my lineage. This time it was on the Leininger side of the family. At a small frontier settlement near Penn's Creek in Central Pennsylvania, Sebastian Leininger and his oldest son were killed by raiding Indians on October 16, 1755. Two daughters - Regina, nearly ten and Barbara, age twelve - were bound and dragged into the wilderness. When the mother and younger son, came home from the grist mill a few miles away, they found their loved ones dead or missing and everything they owned in ruins. They fled to the Tulpehocken Creek region in Berks County.

The two sisters were separated in captivity. Barbara escaped and returned to civilization in 1759. Regina remained with the Indians until the end of the French and Indian War. Mrs. Leininger contacted Conrad Weiser hoping to get her daughter released by the French. Weiser corresponded with Henry Melchior Muhlenberg, the father of the Lutheran Church in America, who at that time was living in Halle, Germany. This correspondence was used in substantiating the Leininger connection to the story. On a winter day in December 1764, Mrs. Leininger's prayers were answered. Her daughter Regina, along with more than 200 other captives, was brought to Carlisle, Pennsylvania to be reconnected with their families.

Unable to recognize her daughter who was now a young woman (19 years of age), Widow Leininger was asked if there was anything at all that Regina might remember from her childhood. All she could remember was that her daughter had learned several hymns as a child when coming to the New World. And when one of those hymns "Allein und Doch Nicht Ganz Allein" (Alone and Yet Not Alone) was sung by Widow Leininger, mother and daughter were miraculously reunited. The chorus of this hymn is as follows:

Alone and Yet Not Alone
Alone and yet not alone,
am I in solitude though drear.
For when no one seems me to own;
My Jesus will to me be near.
I am with Him and He is with me,
I therefore cannot lonely be.
I therefore cannot lonely be.

What a story! But then, I later discovered another twist to the story that is equally amazing. The Indian chief (sachem) who led the attack on the Leininger Homestead at the Penn's Creek Massacre was named Kick-ke-kne-pa-lin (often written as Kickenpawling), a renowned Shawnee chief who took many scalps. What a strange coincidence that an Indian with a name that included what sounded to some like Pawling killed my Leininger relatives at the Penn's Creek Massacre! Who says history is not personal?

While doing a living history workshop at a conference in Anchorage, Alaska, we visited a restaurant whose interior walls were decorated with antiques from the Gold Rush era. While ordering our meal my wife happened to see a boiler plate hanging on the wall with the name Pawling & Harnischfeger on it. Well, I immediately contacted the owner of the restaurant and asked if he knew anything about the plate. He had no idea where it came from. Then the next day I shared this information with a Fish and Wildlife Service ranger who was also attending the workshop and he told me that he had seen many of these plates all over Alaska. Well, here's the rest of the story. The boiler plates were part of earth moving equipment (i.e. back-fillers, wheel trenchers, shovels, backhoes and draglines) used in searching for gold. Today this firm (founded in 1884) is still highly successful. P&H (for Pawling & Harnischfeger) Mining Equipment is, per their website, a "brand synonymous with productive, reliable mining equipment and rock-solid support for cost-focused mining operations."

And the story goes on and on and on... Who says living history doesn't deserve respect in the field of history? It certainly has connected me to my subject forever. So what are you waiting for? Go ahead and do your genealogy. Your connections to the past are waiting. You too can discover who you are and where you came from and add a whole new dimension to your living history presentations.

CHAPTER SIX

The Mohnton "Club 9" baseball team with my grandfather John B. Pawling standing third from the left in the back row. Can you inherit a love of baseball?

You never know where you will find your family heritage. This antique fire engine drove by while we were watching the "Cheyenne Frontier Days" parade in Cheyenne, WY. Later found out we were related and met our new extended family.

The Henry Pawling Family from the area in New York near Rhinebeck knew of Conrad Weiser (portrayed here by the author). Weiser lived at Livingston Manor, NY as a youth after emigrating to the New World in 1720 with his father and other Germans from the Palatinate.

The grave marker of Regina Leininger (former Indian captive) in Christ Lutheran Church cemetery near Stouchburg, PA.

Daniel Boone, born at this site near Douglassville, PA on November 2, 1734 met my lineage during the Braddock Expedition in July 1754 to eradicate the French from the Ohio River Valley. As a wagoner (teamster) on this expedition, Boone encamped at Pawling's Tavern (near Mercersburg, PA) on the retreat following the failed mission.

CHAPTER SEVEN

WHAT IS THAT IN YOUR HAND?
THE FUTURE OF LIVING HISTORY

Recently I received an e-mail from a very close personal friend who I met through living history. He had just contracted a rare form of cancer and was getting "things in order" before undergoing life threatening surgery. The e-mail basically stated that his upcoming surgery was major stuff and that complications from surgery could include death. He went on to ask me if I would help to coordinate the memorial service and honor him in with a eulogy. He also asked if I would sing a specific song entitled "Keepers of the Gems." This is a song that was written by the History Alive! Boys and sung many times when he was in attendance at our concerts. The request took me by surprise. I knew we were friends and asking me to do this was the greatest honor that could be bestowed on me even though I knew it would be emotionally difficult to do. I e-mailed him back and told him I would be honored to do the service - hopefully later than sooner.

I shared this individual's request with Joe Meck who helped write the lyrics to "Keepers of the Gems." He was shocked. When we wrote it, we had no idea what this song would mean to someone some day. The lyrics are as follows:

Keepers of the Gems

Verse 1:
All around this world there are places we hold dear,
Places near to our soul.
They were made by nature's hand and crafted by man,
Now they're in our hands to hold.

Chorus:
You're my children, you're my friends,
Guardians of the land,
Caring for all that I am.
You're the key to the future and all within.
You are the keepers of the gems.

Verse 2:
As multitudes have come and lived upon this earth,
Some have taken more than they need.
And there's only so much this world can give,
Before it falls to its knees.

Verse 3:
Now I pass onto you this baton of life,
Hold it firm to your heart.
With a passion for life, inspire those to come,
For each generation has its part.

You know, life reminds me of a relay race (as I learned at my father's death in 1985). He happened to be my biggest fan. When my brother and I were planning the arrangements for his funeral, the undertaker placed our father's shoes on the floor in front of us and then said, "you boys sure have big shoes to fill." He wasn't kidding as Dad wore size 14 compared to my size 9. I thought to myself, "You got that right!"

I never heard my father use one curse word in my presence. (I sure wish I could say that.) He led his life by his example. Never did he challenge my decision to want to work in the interpretive/living history field. And boy it hasn't been easy. I think all of us living historians have some common horror story of bouncing across America like a bunch of gypsies in search of a lifestyle worthy of our dedication. My dad died just as I received my first seasonal job as a NPS ranger. Matter of fact, when the news of my dad's pending death came to me I was at work and was told by the secretary of the site that I was to report to the Reading Hospital immediately. I arrived at his bedside with my NPS uniform upon my back and flat hat on my head - the very thing he would have been proud to see me wearing. But it was already too late. He was gone. A wave of emotion swept over me. I felt like I was standing on a beach all alone with a huge tsunami approaching. Questions flooded my mind. How can I get up enough nerve to tell my mother and my brother of his passing? How will I ever live on without him? He always had the right answers to all of my questions. Why God did you have to take him in the middle of me trying to start a new career? And Lord, can't you see I am in the beginning of building a log cabin home. I need Dad now more than ever!

Through the days and years that followed after my father's death I have come to think back to that realization that life is like a big relay race. One generation after another runs the race of life and at the end of life on Earth they pass the baton to the next generation and then cheer for those runners on Earth from a distance. It hit me that we have two choices when dealing with the death of someone who is close to us: 1) We can be bitter and hate forever or... 2) We can honor that individual by dedicating our life to what they taught us and carry on.

In earlier chapters I told you that my dad was an art education professor/teacher and that he loved his God. It has been over 25 years since his death. There are many times when I have been working on a carpentry project at my workbench in the basement and grab a tool that my father once taught me how to use. In those moments, thoughts of him come flooding back to me. I have come to realize that my dad is still watching over me from a distance. He is still teaching me even though he is gone. His words of wisdom,which I thought were stupid when I was a teenager, now become my quotes. He is in me. I can't take that out of me. And that is the beauty of life.

My acceptance speech in 1995 when receiving the "Excellence in Interpretation Award" from the National Association for Interpretation was dedicated to my father. I've copied it below:

To My Friend

People often ask me when I got started in the field of living history? Well it began on March 13, 1951 when I was born! If that is the case, then I have a lot of people to thank for aiding me in winning this "National Award of Excellence" in the field of interpretation.

But there is one person I would like to honor this evening by dedicating this award to him. Even though you have never met this person - you all know him. You see it was this person who taught me the skills which enabled me to win this prestigious award. He taught me to observe and be sensitive of others needs and beliefs. He taught me the value of how to express myself. He said you must know how to write and above all - know how to speak out and stand for what you believe.

It was he who opened my eyes to the creation and taught me about the love of the Creator of Life. It was he who was always there to encourage me when life's road became so rough - years of rambling from one job to another in search of my niche. "Don't worry, some day your boat will come in," he would say. He never questioned my desires or motives and was always there to help move me and my possessions from one residence to another. Little did he know I would move seven times in two years and thirteen times in five years!

You see, he didn't laugh when I told him I wanted to be a ranger/interpreter/living historian and never said, "why don't you give up this quest and get a real job". He taught me that trials and tribulations produce perseverance and that perseverance produces character. It took thirteen years until I finally achieved that full-time ranger status.

In 1985 my friend left this earth and graduated to the true world of higher education. My friend taught for thirty-eight years as a professor of art education and earned college degrees from Kutztown University of Pennsylvania and Columbia University,

New York on the way to earning his Doctorate of Education. When he died, I learned what life is really all about. Life is like a relay race. One generation after another carries the baton of life and passes it on to the next generation at the end of their life span.

Someday when we meet again I am going to tell him what has happened since he passed the baton of life to me. In 1989 I was awarded the Mid-Atlantic Regional Freeman Tilden Award while working at Hopewell Furnace National Historic Site for the National Park Service. That year I traveled to the National Workshop in St. Paul, Minnesota, sponsored by the National Association for Interpretation. Although I did not win the National Freeman Tilden Award, it was there that I met you again, my friend. For you were in the hearts and souls of the people who attended that conference. You see - it was those relationships, with those interpreters from all across the nation which reinforced what you taught me. They have taught me about the sensitivity of life and the value of friendships - that our journey together is what life is all about. What we do is the essence of love and it is that love of life which makes us who we are.

And then, I will tell him that in 1995 those same friends that I met for the first time in St. Paul, six years later honored me with the national award for "Excellence in Interpretation."

Although you never were there to see my successes dear friend, I dedicate this award to you. This year 1995, I have traveled over 20,000 miles on the road completing 361 living history performances for over 98,000 people.

Yes, you were right - someday my ship would come in! Friend I am here to tell you - my ship has come in, and I intend to keep on inspiring others about life until that day when I will pass that baton on to the next generation. This award is dedicated to my best friend, my dad, my earthly father who taught me all about my Heavenly Father. You are my magic!

Life reminds me of a favorite book that I cherish - *Centennial* by James Michener. This book takes you through the history of the fictional town of Centennial, Colorado. But in typical Michener style he starts at the beginning - meaning he begins the story with the dinosaurs roaming the earth. He continues to tell the story of the town through the stories of the people who inhabited it from fur trappers to 20th century ranchers. Each chapter represents the life of a member of the town's history. What a novel way to view life. We are all part of a continuum.

So what is the future of living history? It's staring us right in the face. **It's you** - the people who are involved or thinking about being involved in the field! So many times I look at the people who represent the field and often they are of the older generation. Many of us, when we were younger, had no interest in "history as it was taught in school." But now as we approach that time in life when we are "becoming history," we relish the opportunity to know who we really are. Thus off we go to research our genealogy and try to find out where we came from and who we are. Most recently I have decided to honor my great great grandfather Captain John Davis Pawling by joining the 7th Reserves, Company H (PA 36th Volunteer Regiment),"The Cumberland Guard" reenactment group for the 150th Anniversary of the Civil War. Many units are having trouble filling the ranks. Some have lost members to the hottest new living history trend (interpreting WWII). And others are losing members because the "old" guard is dying off or just can't afford it anymore. It's expensive if done correctly.

Some blame the younger generation for not being responsible and not loving history as our generation loves it. Really??? "All they want to do is watch video games and become couch potatoes. They're all losers," I recently heard a Civil War reenactor say. Well I disagree with that summation of the youth of America. Many are very interested in the past but have no one willing to take the time to teach them that **History is People**. That it's all about **you**! My most recent class of Historic Interpretive Techniques students at Hocking College blew my mind. All fourteen students earned an "A" from Prof "tough on historical accuracy" Pawling. Many of them had no prior experience in living history but they jumped into the course with a passion for learning and for life. It was one of the most fulfilling moments in my career as I got an energy transfusion from my students. It was a symbiotic relationship. You might say - they lived off of me and I lived off of them. All of them are considering pursuing living history in their interpretive careers. God bless them.

I wondered, as I said good-bye to them at the end of the term, if they will run into good mentors or burned out administrators when they began working in the field. Like the parable of the sower of the seeds taught by Jesus Christ. (It is interesting to note that Freeman Tilden considered Jesus Christ the greatest interpreter of all times.) According to Jesus some seeds fell on rocky soil and died and others fell on good soil and bloomed. Remember enthusiasm can be contagious, but lack of enthusiasm is just as motivating (or de-motivating).

The future of living history rests in the hands of my age group. It's our mission to pass the baton to the next generation. Where are those among the new generation who could be filling the ranks of living history future? I realize that history in the public schools is at times "on the ropes." Due to politically correct history and the emphasis on subjects that some administrators have deemed of more value (i.e., language arts, math, and science), history is being crowded out. History has found itself on the "back burner." "If we don't get our students ready for passing the mandatory state tests, we won't receive funding for our school," a teacher told me. This so-called "No Child Left Behind" initiative has turned into "some ignorant ones pushed ahead" instead. When I asked my class of 144 college students at Penn State Berks a few years back how many of them had ever heard of Daniel Boone, only two hands went up. And, those two students had no idea about what he had accomplished concerning American history. (Oh, by the way Daniel's birth place was only ten miles away from that campus.) So a few days later I decided to put the name of George Armstrong Custer on the board and told them that he invented the custard pie. And, to my amazement, my students wrote it down in their notes! Of course, I later retracted that intentional error, explaining that I was hoping that someone would object. No one did! Where is this all going? Is this a generation that doesn't know who they are, because they don't know where they have come from? I wonder - who is at fault? Maybe the answer is all of us - the SAA (Society of Apathetic Americans). Who cares?? Leave me alone! What do I get out of this?

Well, I don't totally agree with that statement either. Many of us have taken the time to make a difference. But think of what we are up against. While passing time in an airport terminal recently, I overheard a mother talking to another mother about her children, "There's basketball practice, football practice, soccer practice, cheerleading practice, choral practice and hockey practice which my kids **need to be involved with** in order to grow up to be well rounded successful Americans." I thought to myself "like wow!!!" Yeah, they will own a big car, big house, big bass boat and have accomplished a big nothingness when their life comes to the end of the road. And, remember that all "of that stuff" can't go with you to the next life.

I am starting to believe that our American infatuation with sports is helping to dumb down our society. Oh, don't get me wrong. I still like to occasionally view a sporting event. I have performed at the National Baseball Hall of Fame many times interpreting the history of baseball. But there needs to be balance in our world. We have been indoctrinated into making sports an American Religion of sorts. We give our offerings to it when we buy tickets to an event. It has its own religious dialect (e.g., D-fence, struck out, three-pointer, hit a grand slam on my first date, it's not over until the fat lady sings, etc.) and its own icons (football jerseys, hats, t-shirts, etc.). It has its own foodways and customs (e.g., hotdogs and beer; tailgating and more beer, painting your face and walking around half naked when the temperature is below 0 degrees at a football game due to more beer, cussin' while spittin' on people around you because of drinkin' more beer, etc.). Can this nation have a sporting event without "more beer?"

When performing at the National Baseball Hall of Fame, a teenager and his father approached me as one of the "Boys of Base Ball" who just got done performing with Ozzie Smith. The kid's question to me was, "Are you important enough to sign me an autograph?" This happened to be the wrong question at the wrong time!! The kid already had his arms full of autographed baseball bats and his Pop looked like he remortgaged the house to pay for his kid's trip to the Hall of Fame. Thus my answer was how much time do you have so I can tell you how important I am? Do you have maybe one day? Two days?? A week?? Well, I went on to explain that I am extremely worthy of an autograph **for I am a teacher**! Because, if it wasn't for a teacher none of these modern day Hall of Famers would be able to add up all of their money. And, if it wasn't for a teacher, they couldn't even read their million dollar contracts. And, if it wasn't for a teacher, they wouldn't be able to drive their "hot" cars or even sign their names (and charge you big bucks to do so). And you ask me whether I am worthy of signing you an autograph? Needless to say he didn't get the autograph, but he sure got a lesson about life!

Keep in mind the simple things in life are still free. It's a matter of priorities. What is that in your hand? Good point! I am speaking to all of us. I believe we are in good hands. I believe the future is bright - even though I am a realist. We are up against a mountain of challenging times. The pay for working in the living history field is way behind that of other professionals of equal status. Many have left the field because they can't afford to stay in it. And then there are those in the living history field who wear the incorrect period clothing, misinterpret American culture and have never gone through half of the educational background that many of us have gone through and believe they are worthy of the same respect and remuneration. I was once told by a visitor that since you enjoy doing living history, you really should not be paid for doing it. Work can never be fun!! And also, who cares if you have any kind of credentials? All you need to work in this field is to have a love for it. Well my response to that statement was, "Do you go to a physician who doesn't have a medical degree for heart surgery, but who loves to operate on people? Well, I deal with keeping America's heart ticking." Patriotism begins with understanding our past - the good, the bad and the ugly.

If we haven't heard enough bad news, there's the daily news media telling us about the looming budget cuts that are coming. And what usually goes first – support for the cultural elements that are the most important to American society. Heritage interpretation has been and will continue to be on "the ropes."

But where there is a will, there is a way! Remember the future of America is resting on our shoulders. **We are the Keepers of the Gems**. So what are you waiting for? Go ahead and put on some historically accurate clothing, do your research and go back to the past by inspiring someone to explore their heritage. **The future begins today.**

CHAPTER SEVEN

The History Alive! Boys recorded this double CD "Live in Danville, PA" where the first T-rail in America was rolled in 1845. Top to bottom on the cover – Joe Meck, Rich Pawling and Van Wagner.

My dad as an art education professor at then Kutztown State Teacher's College (now Kutztown University) in the early 1950s.

Navy Lt. John Allen Pawling responded when his country called for volunteers to serve during WWII.

The love of a grandfather for his first grandchild (Janelle).

Honoring those who served in the Civil War is the 7th Pennsylvania Reserves, Company H of the 36th Volunteer Regiment. "The Cumberland Guard" was reactivated in March of 1975 by individuals in the Mechanicsburg/Harrisburg area interested in studying and preserving our Civil War Heritage.

Instructor Pawling with his all "A" Historic Interpretive Techniques class at Robbins Crossing (Hocking College) in Nelsonville, OH.

Former high school history teacher and "Boys of Base Ball" player Walt Malewicz portraying Hall of Famer Mike "the King" Kelly (a star during the 1880s). This photo was taken next to Kelly's likeness (on the left) in the National Baseball Hall of Fame. Walt is an exact "look-a-like" for "the King."

So…what are you waiting for? Go ahead, put on some historically accurate clothing and go back to the past – the future begins today!

EXHIBIT 1

Sample Living History Character Timeline

Timeline of Booker T. Washington's Life

*   personal information pertaining to Booker T. Washington

1849 California Gold Rush

1850 Fugitive Slave Law enacted

1851 September 11 - Fugitive Slave Rebellion, Christiana, Pennsylvania

1855 Bessemer patents converter for producing cheap steel

1856* April 5 - born in Virginia, a slave; mother a cook (black) and father an unknown white plantation owner

1856 May 24 - John Brown of Osawatomie massacres five pro-slavery men in Kansas; Bleeding Kansas

1857 March 4 - James Buchanan (Lancaster, PA) inaugurated President of USA

1857 March 6 - The U.S. Supreme Court declares that blacks "were not, and had never been intended to be citizens" by the framers of the Constitution; Dred Scott Case

1858 George Pullman invents sleeping car and harvester patented by Charles Wesley Marsh

1858 August 5 - First Atlantic telegraph cable completed

1858 August21-October 15 - Lincoln vs. Douglas Debates

1858 September - Oberlin-Wellington rescue. John, a fugitive Negro is rescued by a crowd of Oberlin students and a professor and sent off to Canada

1859 Gold Rush of 1859 - "Pike's Peak or Bust"

1859 August 27 - First oil strike in U.S. - Titusville, Pa, beginning of modern oil industry

1859 Oct 16-18 - John Brown's raid on Harper's Ferry

1860 March 19 - Elizabeth Cady Stanton addresses a joint session of New York Legislature on woman's suffrage

1861   March 4 - Abraham Lincoln the "Black" Republican is inaugurated President of the United States

1861   April 14 - Ft Sumter surrenders to Confederacy

1861   November 15 – U.S. Christian Commission organized by YMCA for service to Union soldiers.

1862   May 20 - Homestead Act: grants free farm of 160 acres on Western Land to any person who will occupy and improve it for 5 years

1862   President Lincoln is quoted in saying "My paramount object in this struggle is to save the Union, and it is not either to save or destroy slavery"

1863   January 1 - Emancipation Proclamation issued by President Lincoln proclaiming freedom for slaves in states or parts of states in rebellion

1863   July 13-16 - anti-draft mob takes over New York City (Movie: *Gangs of New York*)

1863   July 18 - Colonel Robert Gould Shaw - white man in charge of all black soldiers, (54th Massachusetts) first black regiment from the North to fight; led attack upon Fort Wagner in Charleston Harbor (Movie: *Glory*)

1863   November 19 - Gettysburg Address: all men created equal; "government of the people, by the people, for the people shall not perish from the earth"

1864   "In God We Trust" first appears upon 2-cent piece

1864*   Dr. George Washington Carver was born

1865   April 9 - Lee surrenders to Grant

1865   April 14 - President Lincoln shot by John Wilkes Booth

1865*   Booker's family moves to Malden (near Charleston), West Virginia

1865   December 6 - 13th Amendment of the Constitution abolishing slavery is ratified

1866   Ku Klux Klan organized

1867   Steel rail manufacture in United States begun on a large scale

1868   George Westinghouse perfects air brake, marking the beginning of modern railroad

1868   14th Amendment ratified; all persons born or naturalized in the U.S. entitled to citizenship and equal protection under U.S. laws

1869   May 10 - Transcontinental Railroad completed

1870   January 10 - Standard Oil Company incorporated in Cleveland, Ohio with million dollar capital, John D. Rockefeller a principal incorporator

1870   March 30 - 15th Amendment ratified, giving voting rights to all male citizens regardless of race or former servitude

1872*   Booker enrolls at Hampton Institute

1872   March 1 - Yellowstone National Park established by an act of Congress

1873   Colt Peacemaker and the 1873 Winchester 44-40 Rifle are introduced

1874   Barbed wire invented

1876   June 25 - General George Custer defeated at Little Big Horn

1876   Invention of the telephone

1877   June 21 - Hanging of ten Molly Maguires in one day in Pennsylvania coalfields

1879   Charles Edison invents incandescent lamp

1880   March 1 - Supreme Court holds unconstitutional a West Virginia law excluding Negroes from jury duty

1880   Andrew Carnegie monopolizes the steel industry

1881-1900 23,800 strikes and lockouts recorded in the United States

1881*   July 4 - Tuskegee Institute opened by Booker T. Washington

1881   Gunfight at the O.K. Corral, Tombstone, Arizona

1881   Billy the Kid shot by Pat Garrett in Sumner, New Mexico

1882   Jesse James killed by Robert Ford in St. Joseph, Missouri

1886   Geronimo Surrenders

1886   United States the largest producer of steel in the world

1890   December. 29 - Battle of Wounded Knee

1892   Charles Duryea finishes his gasoline buggy--first American made automobile

1892   July 1-Nov 20 - Homestead Strike. H.C. Frick and Andrew Carnegie

1893   Thomas Edison produces the kinetoscope making motion pictures possible

1893   Henry Ford test drives his first automobile

1895* Atlanta Compromise speech.

1896* Receives honorary Master's Degree from Harvard University

1898-1899   Spanish-American War

1900* *The Story of My Life* published

1901   President McKinley killed; Vice President Teddy Roosevelt becomes President

1901* President Theodore Roosevelt entertains Booker T. Washington at White House (first black to be invited to the White House by the President); results in reprisals against blacks in the South.

1901* *Up from Slavery* first published

1901* Receives honorary Doctorate degree from Dartmouth College

1901   May 12 - beginning of the "long strike". Over 147,000 miners walk out of the coal mines for over 5 months led by Johnny Mitchell United Mine Workers President

1903   December 17 - Orville and Wilbur Wright make first successful airplane flight

1908   Henry Ford's Model T Ford goes on the market at $850.50

1909   NAACP organized under leadership of W.E.B. DuBois

1909* Booker is criticized by W.E.B. Du Bois as the great "Accommodator"

1911*   *My Larger Education* published

1912*   *The Man Farthest Down* published

1915*   Booker speaks out against racist portrayal of blacks in movie "Birth of a Nation"

1915*   November 14 - Booker T. Washington dies at age 59; Tuskegee Institute/University endowment equaled over $1.5 million

1916   National Park Organic Act was passed - creating the National Park Service

1917   United States involvement in WWI begins

1919   19th Amendment ratified allowing women the right to vote

EXHIBIT 2

Who Cares What I Wear?
The Case for Historically Accurate Clothing

Five Things to Consider When Determining the Accuracy of Your Clothing

1. What is my character's exact time period? (narrow to a five year period at minimum if after 1850).

2. What is my character's social status (upper or working class)?

3. What is my character's geographic location?

4. What is my character's ethnic background?

5. What is my budget??

Back-up Documentation – Resources for Researching Period Clothing

1. Accurately dated photographs and postcards.

2. Period newspapers & magazines such as local farm journals, local newspapers, *Demorest's Monthly Magazine* (1864+), *Harper's Bazaar* (1867+) and *Ladies Standard Magazine* (1889-1897)

3. Period diaries (particularly women's diaries describing clothing construction and fabrics).

4. Period patterns/pattern catalogs, for example:

   E. Butterick (begun 1863 with boys clothing; ladies fashions added in 1866)

   McCall's (1870+ in *The Queen* & *McCalls*)

5. Museum clothing collections

6. Authoritative books on the history of fashion, clothing, and textiles, for example:

   Blum, Stella, ed. *Fashions and Costumes from Godey's Lady Book.* New York: Dover, 1974.

   Blum, Stella, ed. *Victorian Fashions and Costumes from Harper's Bazaar: 1867-1898.* New York: Dover, 1985.

   Brown, William L. *Thoughts on Men's Shirts in America 1750-1900.* Gettysburg, PA: Thomas Publications, 1999.

Bryk, Nancy Villa, ed. *American Dress Pattern Catalogs, 1873--1909: Four Complete Reprints*. New York: Dover, 1988.

Dalrymple, Priscilla Harris. *American Costume in Early Photographs* (1840's - 1890's). New York: Dover , 1991.

Gehret, Ellen J. *Rural Pennsylvania Clothing: Being a Study of the Wearing Apparel of the German and English Inhabitants, Both Men and Women, Who Resided in Southeastern PA in the Late 18th and Early 19th Century*. York, PA: George Shumway Publisher, 1976.

Gernsheim, Alison. *Victorian and Edwardian Fashion: A Photographic Survey*. New York: Dover, 1982.

Gorsline, Douglas. *What People Wore: 1,800 from Ancient Times to the Early Twentieth Century* (European and American). New York: Dover, 1980.

Lindmier, Tom. *I See by Your Outfit: Historic Cowboy Gear of the Northern Plains*. Glendo, WY: High Plains Press, 1996.

Severa, Joan. *Dressed for the Photographer: Ordinary Americans and Fashion, 1840-1900*. Kent OH: Kent University Press, 1995.

Trestain, Eileen. *Dating Fabrics: a Color Guide 1800-1960*. Paducah, KY: American Quilter's Society, 1998.

The Workwoman's Guide By a Lady. Originally Published in 1838 in London. Guildford, CT: Opus Publications, 1986.

7. "Sutler" pattern catalogs (beware and compare to other sources)

8. Electronic/Internet resources such as:

    American Memory Collections from the Library of Congress
    http://memory.loc.gov/ (Including 1839-1864 Daguerreotypes Collections, Civil War photographs, etc.)

    Fashion Resources: Clothing & Costume History(Kent State University)
    http://www.library.kent.edu/page/11286

ACKNOWLEDGMENTS

There have been literally hundreds of people who have had a part in the writing of this book. Some I know by name and others I met but never got to know them by their full names. And some I never met but they made a lasting impact on my life - Henry David Thoreau, Enos Mills, Ralph Waldo Emerson, Rosalie Edge, John Muir, Aldo Leopold, Jay Norwood "Ding" Darling, Rachel Carson, Freeman Tilden. I regret that there will be many of you who I should have included but simply forgot to mention. Please forgive me.

Along with the people already mentioned in Chapter Five, listed below are people who are special to me and to whom I owe a great debt of gratitude for teaching me about life:

Matt Riegel - my friend and a fellow living history reenactor. We met at Hopewell Furnace NHS as living history moulders. Matt was chosen to assist with the editing of this book because he is a scholar and a deep thinker who shares my passion for life and what it has to teach us.

Jim Lewars - the former site manager of both the Daniel Boone Homestead and the Conrad Weiser Homestead and now currently the site manager for the Landis Valley Farm Museum. He has been a guiding force in my life and believed in me way back when I first entered the living history field.

Lester Breininger - His redware pottery is known throughout the world. This extraordinary man has dedicated his life to saving the Pennsylvania Dutch culture. He knows Conrad Weiser's life like none other. He is a true inspiration and a valuable educator.

Dr. T. Lindsay Baker – a man of incredible energy and knowledge. His published works are some of the best I have ever read on American History. He and his wife Julie have shared Victorian vacations with Diane and me and it was on one of those events that we became "The Living Dead."

Stan McGee – the commanding officer for the 5th New York Zouaves. A reenactor of the finest caliber as well as being a National Park ranger and a friend. He and his wife Judy have opened their home to Diane and me for some of the best living history "gatherings" we have ever experienced.

Meryl Murphy - a Susquehanna riverman who I met when helping to spray for gypsy moth invasions with the Pennsylvania Bureau of Forestry. A man who was my mentor for a few months and taught me that the smartest men are not always the most formally educated. Education doesn't always come from schools of higher learning. It comes from the heart and a willingness to share.

Carl Graybill - the director of information and education for the Pennsylvania Game Commission in 1995. His leadership saved many a day on the road for me that year. He was always there for support when "Bucky Jones" was down and out.

Mike Schmit - former deputy executive director with the Pennsylvania Game Commission. We met when I was nothing more than a young naturalist who wanted to save the environment. Then many years later, he was a guiding force in the Pennsylvania Game Commission's 100th Anniversary. From the time he was a rookie as a wildlife conservation officer until his retirement as deputy executive director, his words of encouragement have been important to me.

Lamar Bailey - my barber from childhood (back when I had hair) but also a fan of History Alive!. He and his wife Brenda have followed me around the country - always believing in me.

Walt Malewicz - a great road companion and fellow interpreter with History Alive!. Walt was there performing with me from the Baseball Hall of Fame as Mike "The King" Kelly to the bowels of the earth as we represented coal miners - literally the ups and downs of living history! His constant excellence in performance helped make me shine.

Joe Meck - words cannot describe him. No one can out-pick him on a guitar and no one can out-talk him. His jokes have made life entertaining during stressful times on the road and his musical abilities are the best.

Freddy Adam - a Pennsylvania Dutchman of renowned. It was through this nationally known modified stock car legend from Kutztown, Pennsylvania that I met my wife (she was his fan club president). I guess you could say I met her in the "pits." He has been my hero from way back when and continues to amaze me with his knowledge and Pennsylvania Dutch way of thinking.

Scott Kegerise - a true mentor, the kind of friend everyone should have in their lives - willing to tell me the truth when it hurts. He is a real brother who has had the experiences that can give me advice on life. We met through the Reading Buccaneers Sr. Drum and Bugle Corps where we both played first soprano bugle. We are black and blue through and through.

Ron Fink - the best man at my wedding who was with me through **every** situation as we were growing up. During college we were inseparable (just ask his wife Barb!). We shared the good times from little league to ice fishing to hunting camp adventures. He knows me better than anyone (and that is scary!).

Lynn Sprankle - a geography professor who opened my eyes to the connections between American history and the influences of geography upon humanity. Anita (his wife) and Lynn continue to inspire me as we share discoveries about coal mining, logging, the old game refuge days and life in general.

Dr. Dorothy Moyer - my cooperating elementary education teacher in my senior year at Kutztown University who "turned me loose" to become the character I am today. She allowed me to experiment with living history in the classroom. My very first living history attempt was as a Civil War Union soldier returning home from the war. The students ate it up.

Rodney Galentin - A retired coal miner friend from southeast Ohio who has a passion for saving the coal mine heritage of his home town of Buchtel. He took me under his wing during a very stressful period in my life and showed me the value of saving the past for the future.

Dr. Jack Benhart - my graduate advisor and former head of the Geography Department at Shippensburg University of Pennsylvania. He believed in me when no one seemed to care.

Joe Gruse and his family - a coal miner for forty-three years from Portage, PA. He and his son (Joe, Jr.) fell in love with my music at the Blue Knob Bluegrass Festival. Joe Sr. called me his hero, but it was really the other way around. I continue to keep in touch with Joe (Jr) and he always lets me know when it is Johnny Mitchell Day. Long may the Gruses be a guide to living life to the fullest.

Bucky Green - a Pennsylvania mountain man and wood carver extraordinaire, but above all a man who has taught me to love the outdoors. His love Elly has been a big part of "putting up with me and my ways." Love you two always.

Barry Wolfe - a retired Pennsylvania state park manager who gave me a chance to prove myself at Greenwood Furnace State Park when I first started History Alive!. His wife (Kathy) and he even named a room "Rich's Room" in their Greenwood Furnace home. The rest you might say became history – fifteen straight years of making Old Home Days come alive!

Jim Cordek - a true ironman (steelworker) and friend. His wife Robin, an exceptional seamstress of period clothing and Jim, an artisan who specializes in the reproduction of historic candle boxes, have been a constant support to both Diane and me. We also share the love of rooting for Pittsburgh based sports teams - the Steelers, the Pirates, and the Penguins.

Dave Frankfort - my neighbor and fellow "Cadillac cowboy" who has talked me out of many a stupid situation (and I have done the same for him - for the most part). His wife Kathy keeps us both in line. I don't know where I would be without them.

Scott Pawling - My new found lost relative who I met at a state park while talking about my genealogy. He connected me to the Pawling Family (Mike and Connie Pawling) in Cheyenne, Wyoming. Along with his wife Tracy they are raising a great family (Reed, Braydon, Miranda, and Carissa).

Van Wagner - A former PSU student and History Alive! Boy who inspired me to learn how to play acoustic instruments. Now he inspires students of his own.

Janelle (Pawling) Matz – my niece, also a teacher, who helped produce many of the photos found in this book. Family is very important in carrying the torch of educational excellence from one generation to another. Many years ago I held her in my arms and now she helps carry me - not in her arms (for I am built like a Sherman tank) but with her abilities.

BIBLIOGRAPHY

Alderson, William T. and Shirley Payne Low. *Interpretation of Historic Sites,* 2nd Edition. Nashville, TN: American Association for State and Local History, 1987.

Alford, Terry. *Prince Among Slaves.* New York, NY: Oxford University Press USA, 1977.

Anderson, Jay. *A Living History Reader, Volume 1 - Museums.* Nashville, TN: American Association for State and Local History, 1991.

Anderson, Jay. *The Living History Sourcebook.* Nashville, TN: American Association for State and Local History, 1985.

Anderson, Jay. *Time Machines - The World of Living History.* Nashville, TN: American Association for State and Local History, 1984.

Baker, Dr. T. Lindsay. "Why This Professor Loves Living History" Association for Living History, Farm and Agricultural Museums Vol. XXXVIX, No. 2, Summer 2009.

Beck, Larry and Ted Cable. *Interpretation for the 21st Century: Fifteen Guiding Principles for Interpreting Nature and Culture.* Champaign, IL: Sagamore Publishing, 1998.

Brochu, Lisa and Tim Merriman. *Personal Interpretation: Connecting Your Audience to Heritage Resources.* Fort Collins, CO: National Association for Interpretation, 2008.

Browne, Walter A. *The American Development.* Kirksville, Missouri: Simpson Printing & Publishing Company, 1964.

Carson, Barbara G. and Cary Carson. *Interpreting the Historical Scene.* Nashville, TN: American Association for State and Local History for the National Park Service, 1988.

Carson, Barbara G., and Cary Carson. "Things Unspoken: Learning Social History from Artifacts." In *Ordinary People and Everyday Life: Perspectives on the New Social History,* edited by James B. Gardner and G. Rollie Adams, 181-203. Nashville, TN: American Association for State and Local History, 1983.

Carson, Cary. "Living Museums of Everyman's History" *Harvard Magazine* 83 (July-August 1981): 22-32.

Coombs, Barry B. *Westward to Promontory: Building the Union Pacific Across the Plains and Mountains.* New York: Crown Publishers, 1969.

Deetz, James. *In Small Things Forgotten - The Archeology of Early American Life.* Garden City, NY: Anchor Press, 1977.

Ecroyd, Donald H. *Living History.* Fort Washington, PA: Eastern National Park and Monument Association, 1990.

Frye, Melinda Young. "Costume as History." *Museum News* 56 (November-December 1977): 37-42.

Gardner, James B. and George Rollie Adams. *Ordinary People and Everyday Life: Perspectives on the New Social History.* Nashville, TN: American Association for State and Local History, 1983.

Geographic Perspectives on America's Past: Readings on the Historical Geography of the United States. Edited by David Ward. New York, NY: Oxford University Press, 1979.

Gerlach, Larry R. "Viewpoint: Making the Past Come Alive." *History News* 30 (September 1975): 222-225.

Grater, Russell K. *The Interpreter's Handbook: Methods, Skills, and Techniques.* Tucson, AZ: Southwest Parks and Monument Association, 1976.

Gutman, Herbert G. *Who Built America? Volume One.* New York: Pantheon Books, 1989.

Gwaltney, William W. "Journeys of the Mind: the Future of Living History" *The Interpreter Magazine.* (Spring 1983).

Hadden, R. Lee. *Reliving the Civil War: A Reenactor's Handbook.* Mechanicsburg, PA: Stackpole Books, 1996.

Haas, Irvin. *America's Historic Villages and Restorations.* New York: Arco Publishing, 1974.

Hahn, Thomas F. *The C&O Canal: Pathway to the Nation's Capital.* Metuchen, NJ: Scarecrow Press, 1984.

Hilker, Gordon. *The Audience and You.* Washington, DC: U.S. Department of Interior/National Park Service Office of Publications, 1974.

Hindle, Brooke and Steven Lubar. *Engines of Change: the American Industrial Revolution 1790-1860*. Washington, DC: Smithsonian Institution Press, 1986.

Horn, Marilyn J. *The Second Skin: An Interdisciplinary Study of Clothing*. Boston: Houghton Mifflin, 1975, 1-6.

Kay, William Kennon. *Keep It Alive - Tips on Living History Demonstrations*. Washington, DC: U.S. Department of Interior/National Park Service Office of Publications, 1970.

Klein, Maury. *Union Pacific:The Birth of a Railroad 1862-1893*. New York: Doubleday, 1987.

Knudson, Douglas, Ted Cable and Beck, Larry. *Interpretation of Cultural and Natural Resources*. 2nd edition. State College, PA: Venture Press, Inc. 2003.

Korson, George. *Pennsylvania Songs and Legends*. Baltimore: John Hopkins Press, 1949, 447.

Kytle, Elizabeth. *Home on the Canal*. Cabin John, MD.: Seven Locks Press, 1983.

Kyvig, David E. and Myron A. Marty. *Nearby History*. Nashville, TN: American Association for State and Local History, 1982.

Laslett, John. *The Workingman in American Life*. Boston: Houghton Mifflin Company, 1968.

Lewis, David W. *Iron and Steel in America*. Greenville, DE: Hagley Museum, 1976.

Lewis, Pierce F. "Axioms for Reading the Landscape: Some Guides to the American Scene" In *The Interpretation of Ordinary Landscapes*. Edited by D.W. Meinig. New York: Oxford University Press, 1979, 11-32.

Lewis, William J. *Interpreting for Park Visitors*. Philadelphia, PA: The Acorn Press, 1981.

Licht, Walter. *Working for the Railroad*. Princeton, NJ: Princeton University Press, 1983.

Mackintosh, Barry. *Interpretation in the NPS: A Historical Perspective*. Washington, DC: U.S. Department of Interior/National Park Service Office of Publications, 1986.

McCutcheon, Marc. *The Writer's Guide to Everyday Life in the 1800's*. Cincinnati,OH: Writer's Digest Books, 1993.

McDaniel, George W. *Hearth and Home: Preserving a People's Culture*. Philadelphia. PA: Temple University Press, 1981, 149-186.

Meaningful Interpretation: How to Connect Hearts and Minds to Places, Objects, and Other Resources. Edited by David L. Larson, Fort Washington, PA: Eastern National, 2003.

Michener, James A. *Centennial.* New York, NY: Random House, 1974.

Miller, Donald L. and Richard E.Sharpless. *The Kingdom of Coal: Work, Enterprise, and Ethnic Communities in the Mine Fields.* Philadelphia, PA: University of Pennsylvania Press, 1985.

Mills, Enos. *Adventures of a Nature Guide: and Essays in Interpretation.* Edited by Edna Mills. Friendship, WI: New Past Press, Inc. 1990.

O'Connell, Peter S. "Putting the Historic House into the Course of History." *Journal of Family History* 6 (Spring, 1981), 28-40.

Pawling, Albert Schoch. *Pawling Genealogy.* Originally published in Lewisburg, PA, 1905. Revised Addition 1905 to 1984 by Harold M. Danowsky.

Pawling, Richard Nelson. "Geographical Influences on the Development and Decline of the Union Canal" *Proceedings of the Canal History and Technology Symposium.* Volume Two (March 26, 1983), 69-85.

Pawling, Richard Nelson. *A Historic Survey of Swatara State Park.* Harrisburg, PA: Pennsylvania Bureau of State Parks, 1981.

Pawling, Richard Nelson. "Interpreting America's Forgotten Hero: The Common Laborer" *1990 National Interpreter's Workshop Proceedings.* Fort Collins: National Association for Interpretation, 1990, 208-210.

Pawling, Richard Nelson. "Lower Reaches of the Tulpehocken" *Historical Review of Berks County* (Summer 1983), 86-120.

Pawling, Richard Nelson. "Slow Boat to Birdsboro" *Historical Review of Berks County* (Summer 1984), 110-121.

Pawling, Richard Nelson. "The Union Canal in Berks County" *Historical Review of Berks County* (Summer 1982), 98-117.

Pawling, Richard N. "Where We Have Come From and Where We Are Going: The Philosophy of Interpretation" *Legacy* 3 (March/April 1992), 16-19.

Porter, Glen. *The Worker's World at Hagley.* Wilmington, DE: Eleutherian Mills-Hagley Foundation, 1981.

Rentzhog, Sten. *Open Air Museums: the History and Future of a Visionary Idea.* Translated by Skans Victoria Airey. Published in cooperation with the Association for Living History, Farm and Agricultural Museums. Sweden: Jamtli Forlag and Carlsson Bokfortag, 2007.

Rollins, Barbara Breedlove. "The Pawling Family" in Barbara Breedlove Rollins' Family Files. Http:www.sharpwriters.com/genealogy/pawling.html (accessed February 5, 2008)

Roth, Stacy F. *Past into Present: Effective Techniques for First-Person Historical Interpretation.* Chapel Hill: University of North Carolina Press, 1998.

Savage, Lon. *Thunder in the Mountains: the West Virginia Mine War 1920-21.* Pittsburgh, PA: University of Pittsburgh Press, 1990.

Severa, Joan. "Authentic Costuming for Historic Site Guides" Technical Leaflet 111, Nashville: American Association for State and Local History, 1979.

Sharpe, Grant W. *Interpreting the Environment.* New York: John Wiley & Sons, 1976.

Shaw, Ronald E. *Canals for a Nation: The Canal Era in the United States 1790-1860.* Lexington, KY: University Press of Kentucky, 1990.

Sherfy, Marcella. "The Craft of History" *In Touch: the Interpreters Information Exchange 13,* (May 1976), 4-7.

Stover, John F. *History of the Baltimore and Ohio Railroad.* West Lafayette, IN: Purdue University Press, 1987.

Sullivan, William. *The Industrial Worker in Pennsylvania 1800-1840.* Harrisburg, PA.: Pennsylvania Historical and Museum Commission, 1855.

Tales the Boatmen Told. Edited by James Lee. Easton, PA: Delaware Press, 1991.

Taylor, Dale. *The Writer's Guide to Evryday Life in Colonial America: From 1607-1783.* Cincinnati, OH: Writer's Digest Books, 1997.

Tilden, Freeman. *Interpreting Our Heritage.* Chapel Hill: Uni. of North Carolina Press, 1957.

Tilden, Freeman. *Interpreting Our Heritage.* 4th edition, expanded and updated. Chapel Hill, NC: University of North Carolina Press, 2007.

Tilden, Freeman. *The National Parks: What They Mean to You and Me.* New York, NY: Alfred A. Knopf, 1951.

Tobin, Catherine. "Irish Labor on American Canals" *Canal History and Technology Proceedings*. Volume IX (March 17, 1990), 163-189.

Tobin, Catherine. *The Lowly Muscular Digger: Irish Canal Workers in 19th Century America*. Notre Dame, IN.: University of Notre Dame Ph.D. Dissertation, 1987.

Walker, Joseph E. *Hopewell Village: The Dynamics of a 19th Century Iron-Making Community*. Philadelphia, PA: University of Pennsylvania Press, 1966.

ABOUT THE AUTHOR

Rich Pawling is the owner and educational/interpretive specialist of **History Alive!**^{SM} - a firm founded in 1991 that provides living history and traditional/heritage music programs and training workshops to parks, museums, and universities as well as civic, professional and historical organizations throughout the United States and Canada.

Following employment as an environmental educator for state parks and a historian-naturalist for county parks, Rich was employed from 1984-1990 as a National Park Ranger assigned to Hopewell Furnace National Historic Site. His NPS accomplishments include the creation and design of the first person (living history) programming at Hopewell Furnace and winner of the Freeman Tilden Award ("Interpreter of the Year") for the Mid-Atlantic Region of the National Park Service. In 1991, he founded **History Alive!** and returned to adjunct college teaching as a cultural geography professor. In both 1993 and 2002, he was awarded the "Outstanding Adjunct Professor of the Year Award" at Penn State Berks. Other educational honors include: winner of the Kutztown University Rothermel Alumni Award, named one of KU"s "100 Most Distinguished Alumni of the 20th Century" and selection for *Who's Who Among America's Teachers* and *Who's Who in America* (Marquis). He has taught various courses including Cultural Geography, Human Geography, Geography of North America, Geographic Influences on American History, Introduction to Geography, Planet Earth, Introduction to Geology, Meteorology, Man and the Biosphere and Pennsylvania German Culture of the Sectarians at five Pennsylvania colleges/universities: Penn State, Millersville University, Albright College, Reading Area Community College. He most recently taught full-time as a professor at Hocking College (located in Nelsonville, Ohio) in the Natural Resources Department - teaching courses in Interpretive Methods, Historic Interpretive Techniques and Essentials in Geology.

Paralleling his teaching career, his national reputation of excellence in living history grew and in 1995, Rich was the winner of the National Association for Interpretation (NAI) "Excellence in Interpretation Award" (presented at the annual workshop at Disney World in Orlando, FL). This is a national distinction presented annually to one individual, institution or agency that has "displayed excellence in the practice of frontline field interpretation and, through their efforts, have influenced others." He is currently certified through NAI as a "Certified Interpretive Trainer", a "Certified Interpretive Guide," and a "Sanctioned Trainer of Certified Interpretive Guides." In 2003 he won the NAI Media Award for an "Outstanding Feature Article" for his article on the interpretation of baseball entitled *For the Love of the Game, Interpreting Base Ball.* He is also the "father" of the Cultural

Interpretation and Living History section for NAI. He has frequently served as a judge for National History Day competitions - judging both individual and group living history presentations.

Annually, he presents numerous **History Alive!** performances and living history workshops. In 1995, he took a year's leave of absence from teaching to design and present 220 dramatic/multimedia performances of "100 Years of Wildlife Conservation" for the Pennsylvania Game Commission (PGC). Due the heralded success of the PGC program, he was subsequently contracted to design and perform similar programs for the centennials of Maryland's Natural Resources Police (1996) and the Colorado Division of Wildlife(1997).

Other specially designed programs include acoustic heritage music programs and the company's **Boys of Base Ball.** The former combines historical introductions to the lyrics of the songs of our nation's past - along with accompaniment on a variety of acoustic instruments including mandolin, guitar, dobro, banjolin, and harmonica. The latter, a unique look at baseball's past designed for minor and major league ballparks, was featured at the National Baseball Hall of Fame in 2002 (for Ozzie Smith's Induction), in 2007 (for Cal Ripkin Jr and Tony Gwinn's Induction) and in 2004 for the Hall of Fame Game (Atlanta Braves vs. Minnestoa Twins) Weekend. The "Boys" also performed at both the 2000 (Dallas, TX) and 2002 (Nashville, TN) Baseball Winter Meetings as well as the 2004 Little League World Series (Williamsport, PA).

The company trademark **History is People!**® can be found on products including two music CDs - *History Thru Song* and *Hammered in Iron: Railroad Songs & Stories* by Rich Pawling's History Alive! Boys. Two video titles have been released in a series which focuses on the working class and their role in American history - *Buildin' the Rails: the Life of a Gandy Dancer* (which aired on the History Channel) and *Fire in the Hole! A Coal Miner's Story*. He has written and published the following songs: *Keepers of the Gems, Teaching My Mules the Rules, A Tree Army Man, Conrad Weiser: Never a Man like Him, Bloody Harlan, Laurel Country, The Mighty Iron Men* and *Hammered Out of Love*.

Rich's graduate education, a Master of Science in Geoenvironmental Sciences, was awarded at Shippensburg University of Pennsylvania. His undergraduate degree was completed at Kutztown University of Pennsylvania - majoring in education, environmental science and geography. Rich has authored three historical dramas - one on the history of Ephrata (PA) entitled *The Ephrata Story: Schmutz, Bellyguts, and the Dragon*, another on the oil industry - *Oil on the Brain: The Story of Pennsylvania's Early Oil Days* and one about the surveying of the border between Pennsylvania and Maryland/Delaware - *A Line for Times: the Mason-Dixon Line*. His other written publications include "Geographic Influences on the Development and Decline of the Union Canal" in the *Proceedings of the Canal History and Technology Symposium*; "Hopewell Furnace: A Microcosm of America's 18th and 19th Century Cold Blast Charcoal Iron Industry" in the *Pennsylvania Geographical Society*. In addition, papers published in *National Association for Interpretation Workshop Proceedings* include "Interpreting America's Forgotten Hero: The Common Laborer," "Back on the Road Again - Living History Off-site," "Getting It Right: Excellence in Living History," " Interpreting History Through Song" and "Hurrah for Our National Game: the Interpretation of Baseball." "Where We Have Come From, Where We Are Going: The Philosophy of Interpretation" and the award-winning "For the Love of the Game:

Interpreting Baseball" was published in *Legacy* magazine (NAI).

Rich Pawling's **History Alive!** has presented interpretive living history programs or training sessions throughout the United States and Canada including: the Colorado Historical Society (Denver, CO), Colorado State University (Fort Collins, CO), Delaware State Parks, Maryland State Parks, California State Parks, National Baseball Hall of Fame (Cooperstown, NY), Palatines to America Annual Conference, Historic Southern Indiana, Pennsylvania State Parks, the PA Game Commission, PA Historical and Museum Commission, U.S. Forest Service (Portland, OR), New River Gorge National River (Lansing, WV), F.E. Warren AFB, "Fort Russell Days" (Cheyenne, WY), Fort Abraham Lincoln State Park (Mandan, ND), Fort Laramie NHS (Ft. Laramie, WY), Kansas State Museum, Oregon Trail Interpretive Center (Baker City, OR), Rocky Mountain NP (CO), Bent's Old Fort NHS (La Junta, CO), Little Bighorn NB (Crow Indian Agency, MT), Grand Canyon NP (AZ), Havre de Grace Decoy Festival (MD), National Envirothon (University of Pittsburgh, Johnstown, PA), The Wildlife Society National Conference (Snowmass, C0), the Maryland Forest Association (Solomons, MD), New Jersey State Parks, Parks Canada/Fort Wellington, Upper Canada Village (Morrisburg, ON).

He has presented papers at numerous professional association conferences including the American Association for State and Local History (Columbus, OH, Pittsburgh, PA and Denver, CO), the Association for Living History, Farm, and Agricultural Museums (Troy, NY, Hiram, OH, Princeton, NJ, Old Sturbridge Village, MA and Historic Jackson's Mill (Weston, WV), and the National Association for Interpretation (Vail, CO, Charleston, SC, Santa Clara, CA, Washington, DC, Cleveland, OH, Orlando, FL, Billings, MT, Beaumont, TX, Anchorage, AK, Syracuse, NY, Des Moines, IA, Wichita, KS, and Virginia Beach, VA) as well as NAI/CILH Section Workshops (St. Louis and Portland, OR).

One of the many faces of Rich Pawling – author and professor.

Rich Pawling as 1869 Cincinnati Red Stockings feeder/hurler Asa "the Count" Brainard at the National Baseball Hall of Fame (Cooperstown, NY)

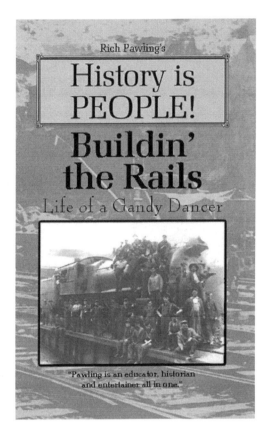

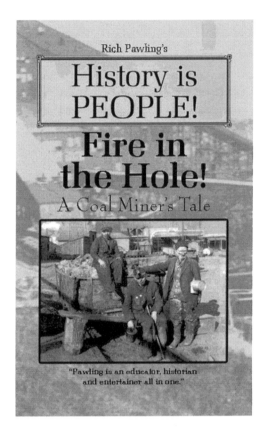

Two of our products carrying our History is People!® trademark.

These videos were originally filmed by Time Warner Video (now distributed by Turning Point Media). See www.richpawling.com for ordering information.

A scene from the historic drama "The Ephrata Story: Schmutz, Bellyguts and the Dragon" (written by Rich Pawling).

The play set with author Rich Pawling for the historical drama, "Oil on the Brain: the Story of Pennsylvania's Early Oil Days."

We are the Keepers of the Gems.

So what are you waiting for?
Go ahead and put on some historically accurate clothing, do your research
and go back to the past by inspiring someone to explore their heritage.

The future begins today.

Made in the USA
Charleston, SC
12 November 2011